Boots to
FREEDOM

Amazing journeys of a woman in her
seventies who found freedom trekking
in different parts of the world

CLAUDE TRANCHANT

Author: Claude Tranchant

ISBN (paperback) 978-0-648-86700-5
ISBN (e-book/epub) 978-0-6488670-1-2

© Copyright 2020

All rights reserved throughout the world. No part of this publication may be reproduced, stored in a retrieval system or transmitted, in any form or by any means, electronic, mechanical, photocopying, recording or otherwise, without the prior written permission and exclusive authorization of the author.

Cataloguing-in-Publication entry is available from the National Library of Australia. http://catalogue.nla.gov.au/

Cover photo: Tyler Nix

Some of the names have been changed to protect privacy.

*I am dedicating this book
to my children Sabine and David,
to my son and daughter in law
Brett and Alexandra, my grand-children
Alexander, Amélie, Harrison and Xavier,
my friends and all the readers of my
previous book 'Boots to Bliss'
as their beautiful and inspiring
comments encouraged me to
write my second book.*

CONTENTS

PROLOGUE   Page 3

CHAPTER 1   Page 6
    Walking with a group in Australia

Larapinta Trail – Red Centre – Australia – The End To End
16 days: 223 kilometres of adventure in the wilderness
30 May 2016 - 14 June 2016 at 70 years of age.

CHAPTER 2   Page 68
    Walking with a group in Nepal

Poon Hill – 3,210 Metres Altitude – Nepal
12 days: Nepal tour/trek - 55 kilometres trekking - Plus tours
6 November 2017 - 17 November 2017 at 71 years of age.

CHAPTER 3   Page 136
    Walking with a Camino Skies' group in Spain

The Camino Frances – Saint-Jean-Pied-De-Port –
Santiago de Compostela
34 days: 12 April 2018 - 17 May 2018 at 72 years of age

CHAPTER 4   Page 248
Walking alone in Spain

Finisterre – Muxia – Dumbria – Santiago de Compostela
10 days: 18 May 2018 - 28 May 2018 at 72 years of age

CHAPTER 5   Page 278
Walking alone in Spain and Portugal

Herbon - Padron - Galandas - Santiago de Compostela
3 days: 30 May 2018 - 1 June 2018 at 72 years of age.

Visiting, walking and travelling in and around Fatima – Porto
5 days: 2 June 2018 - 6 June 2018 at 72 years of age.

CHAPTER 6   Page 296
Walking alone or with a group?

EPILOGUE   Page 304

ACKNOWLEDGEMENT   Page 306

Machhapuchhare Peak - Nepal

अन्नपूर्ण संरक्षण क्षेत्रमा यहाँहरुलाई हार्दिक स्वागत छ !
WELCOME TO
ANNAPURNA CONSERVATION AR
(PLEASE FOLLOW CONSERVATION AREA - CODE OF CONDUCT.)
NTNC-AC

When we are young the days
seem never ending, as we age,
suddenly they become shorter.

Life is long, and life is short.

It all depends on how we walk it or,
and how we feel about it.

At times, we are happy, if someone
gives us a bit of attention.

At times, when we are lonely and
closed up within ourselves, we feel empty,
isolated and so sad.

Eventually, we decide not to let the
sadness overpower us and we take to
the road with a backpack, and
two trekking poles as companions.

As we take to the road, along our
life journey on this earth, a new path
opens in front of us and, somehow,
we find freedom, happiness
and we return renewed.

My backpack

PROLOGUE

The world can be harsh to many who have suffered at the hands of others, either physically or emotionally. The emotional pains are the hardest to deal with; the judgement projected by others, without knowing the person, the misunderstanding of words or perception. One human being may think that someone is weaker or stronger than them. How wrong can one be! Every single being (soul) has his own challenges and has to walk his own path. No one is better or worse than anybody else. We are here on this earth to learn, to grow, to love. And, if at the hand of someone we have felt pain, sorrow, hurt, either willingly or unwillingly, we will have to learn and find a way to let go and eventually to forgive. There are many ways to release our pain. For some odd reason, I was lead to find freedom: walking.

Later in life, at the age of 64, I discovered how to release my emotional pain as I left Brisbane (Australia) with my backpack and my two trekking poles as companions, leaving my somewhat comfortable life to the unknown, as I had never trekked before.

Walking 100 days, alone, along the Saint James' Way, had allowed me to heal, grow and move on. The Saint James' Way is commonly known, in Spain, as the Camino. I started my pilgrimage from Vezelay, a small village in the Northern Central France and finished, 100 days later, at Muxia – Galicia – Spain. I had walked nearly 2,500 kilometres. On my return, I was a new person who believed in herself, her strength, and her abilities to walk the rest of her journey on this earth and to live it to the fullest.

Why was I called to the Camino? At the time, I did not know. Over the years, I had received many signposts, messages, till one day the penny dropped and I decided to challenge myself no matter what. There was a reason why I was directed to walk it from Vezelay and I had to find out why. I had to do the unthinkable so I could finally find freedom and release my heavy heart.

As I was walking day in and day out, I discovered that this path was a blessing, so I could deal with my sadness and my emotional pain. On my return to Australia, after soul searching and with the kind and wise words of a friend, I discovered that I could help others in different ways.

One way was through my writing. This is my journey on various paths across different countries after my first Camino.

From these experiences and various coincidences, I embarked on three different journeys, not alone but with three different groups:

Age 70 – I trekked along the Larapinta trail in the Red Centre of Australia: 'The end to end' which is one of the hardest trails, under foot, in Australia – recorded as the 20th hardest trail in the world

Age 71 – I trekked in Nepal – the Poon Hill Trail to reach an altitude of 3,210 metres

Age 72 – I walked, again, the Saint James' Way in Spain, from Saint Jean Pied de Port – France - to Santiago with the Camino Skies' group for a documentary about the Camino Frances, then from Finisterre, I walked alone to Muxia – Galicia – Spain and returned on foot to Santiago, along the Dumbria Path as well as a small section of the Portuguese Way

Here are my stories.

CHAPTER 1

Walking with a group in Australia

Larapinta Trail – Red Centre – Australia – The End To End

16 days: 223 kilometres of adventure in the wilderness

30 May 2016 - 14 June 2016

at 70 years of age

F irstly, as a tradition in Australia, I want to acknowledge our traditional owners and country.

I acknowledge and pay my respects to the Arrernte and Roulpmaulpma traditional custodians of the lands and waterways of the MacDonnell Ranges where the Larapinta trail crossed their land and thank them for their continued hospitality.

I want to acknowledge and celebrate the continuation of a living culture that has a unique role in this region. I also acknowledge Elders past and present as well as our emerging leaders of tomorrow and thank them for their wisdom and guidance as we walk in their footsteps. Let us hold this tradition in trust as we work and serve our communities for a more just future.

The Larapinta Trail is found in the heart of Australia called the Red Centre, and follows the West MacDonnell Ranges, not far from Alice Springs. It is a wild, scenic, fascinating landscape and a very arid region. The Aborigines, nomadic tribes, have been living in the MacDonnell Ranges for thousands of years. They were hunter-gatherers, and water was very crucial for their survival. Thanks to the permanent water along the MacDonnell Ranges they were able to live there and still do to this day. We would be crossing the tribal lands of the Arrernte and Roulpmaulpma people who had lived here for thousands of years. It was an incredible opportunity equal to none to be able to walk on this ancient trail.

I was very surprised to see how well the Larapinta Trail was signed. You can walk it alone, though it is not recommended. If you are planning to walk it alone, it is paramount to organise your trip well. You will need to plan your food drops along the way, and carry your food and water for a few days at a time as well as camping gear. At campsites, you will find water tanks or reticulated bore water. It is very important to carry more water with you, just in case. In some campsites, along the path, you might find free gas barbecues and water as well. It is wise to treat the water by filtering or using tablets. You will need to be self-sufficient. If you want to walk the Larapinta with an organised group you will find plenty of companies doing so. You will enjoy many sleeps in a swag and under the stars. If you are walking it alone or with friends and find the length of each section too long, you can divide some sections and do them, in two days.

On 29 May 2016, I flew from Brisbane airport to Alice Springs.

In the plane, I recalled what lead me to walk the Larapinta Trail.

At the age of 68, after the launch of my first book, 'Boots to Bliss' from a check out chick (console operator) I had become a self-publisher. My book was among the Best Sellers in various bookstores in Brisbane, and has had some success in other states of Australia, and was read all around the world. I was swept off my feet and this led me to new opportunities for a more fulfilling life. Though I received so much love from others, and my heart was full, I needed some time away to find again, the little Claude, as my darling Maman used to call me. What a good way to go walkabout, alone in the heart of Australia!

In April 2014, I arrived at the backpacker centre, 'Ayers Rock', settled down, and got everything ready for my first walk the next morning as I was going to walk around Uluru (Ayers Rock). Out of respect for our traditional owners, I did not climb Uluru which is a sacred place for Aborigines. Its perimeter is about 12 kilometres. Since 26 October 2019, Uluru cannot be climbed any more. While I was walking, I felt its energy and for some odd reason, I needed to touch the rock, all the time, not understanding why, when high at the top of a peak of this sacred mountain, I saw a perfectly heart-shape. The heart was the symbol of my Camino. I smiled, and saw a sign in this heart. The following day, I walked the Kata Tjuta – Valley of the Winds - (ex-The Olgas). There, I felt a stronger connection with this mountain and understood why, later on, when I learnt that the Kata Tjuta was the mountain for women, Uluru being the mountain for men. Kata Tjuta was magical for me. It felt so good, and an immense sense of peace enveloped me. I would have stayed forever. In the evening, I had the joy of meeting a French couple who were visiting Australia. Therefore, a bit like my first Camino, I joined them for an evening meal and shared time with them under the sky in front of the Uluru Rock with its magical colour at sun down. The next day, and the following days, I trekked, alone, around Uluru and its surrounds, and sat in front of magical sceneries that you can only find in the Australian outback. I bathed in the quietness of nature, away from the busyness of my somewhat hectic life in the city, embracing the beauty, and peacefulness of this mountain. I was wrapped up in an incredible energy like a cloak. It was not a 'déjà vu', it was much more powerful.

A few days later I joined a group. We climbed Kings Canyon, and other mountains. What happened during one of these treks would lead me to the Larapinta Trail 'The End to End'. We were in Redbank, when I needed to touch the side of that mountain. What followed surprised me to the fullest. As I touched the rock, tears started to flow down my cheeks, I could not stop them. I do not know how long it lasted, but some members of the group noticed what was happening. All my body was shaking. It was so eerie and so hard to understand. I separated myself from the group and walked ahead. I did not want to talk to anyone, I was fearful of being judged when one member of the group, Michael, joined me and asked me: 'What happened at Redbank when you touched the rock, Claude?' I was hesitant to share what had occurred, fearful that Michael thought I was mad. My mind was in turmoil. Could I take the risk of sharing this incredible feeling when I could not understand it myself? After a little while, still shaken, I took courage and decided to tell Michael: 'Well, when I placed my hands on the rock, I felt an unexplainable sensation that took over my whole body, and then I heard crying, terrible cries of despair, like coming from the centre of the earth. I do not know if these cries came from our Traditional Owners or the pain of our disturbed world'.

Still scared about what Michael would be thinking, I looked ahead and started to create, in my head, my own little scenario: 'Michael must be thinking that I am probably mad and after all maybe I am'. How can anyone know really?' Michael's reply totally surprised me and left me speechless, as he said: 'some people are more sensitive than others, Claude'.

Later on, I learnt that Michael was a radiologist and maybe, he too, had seen strange (!!) things when he was working with his x-ray equipment. I was still trying to comprehend what had just happened when I saw a signpost with the following words: 'Section 11 and Section 12'. Curiosity arose, and later on I asked about it and learnt that it was the Larapinta Trail 'The End to End', without pondering about it: I said: 'Well Larapinta will see me on my 70th birthday'. Being a person who always keeps her promises to others as well as myself, here I was, two years later, flying again to Alice Springs, Central Australia, on the verge of starting a new adventure, the second long walking adventure in my entire life but with a group this time.

As I arrived at the hotel in Alice Springs, I took possession of my room and walked around the centre of town. I had a somewhat unsettling night. I am sure you can imagine how my mind was unsettled: I was going to walk not alone, but with a group for sixteen days, not one day or two. My mind was restless.

The next morning, I went downstairs for breakfast, and after collecting my backpack, I waited outside the hotel, well before 7.30am to be picked up. To my disbelief, it was raining and the river was very high. I was in the Red Centre of Australia. It was winter! What a start!

Larapinta Trail - Australia

The 4WD arrived, with nearly all the members of the group. After a brief 'Hi', and acknowledgement from only one member, I sat at the back of the vehicle and with a smile on my face, I observed the other members of the group. They looked quite sporty, seasoned walkers and all much younger than me. 'OMG Claude, what have you put yourself in for? A bit late girl! Oh well here you are, here you go'.

We arrived at the historic Alice Springs Telegraph Station, official start of the trail, situated at the North of Alice Springs Town. Our guides, Rose and Archer, introduced themselves, and showed us the map of the whole trek. I listened to what was said, but I did not realise nor comprehend, what was ahead of me.

Then we started walking, following the Old Telegraph line, crossing granite ridges which were quite slippery due to the recent rain. We crossed the famous Australian Ghan Railway lines, and climbed the high escarpments to the top of the Euro Ridge. What Euro Ridge? I thought Euro was the European currency. Well, I had better enquire about that one! Euro Ridge had nothing to do with the Euro currency. For our traditional owners, the highest peak represents the head and back of a 'Euro', an ancestor who stopped there and while digging for water created a waterhole. For the traditional owners, his spirit still remains there.

Archer was carrying our lunch in his huge backpack. I thought: It is nice to be strong and young! This section was challenging not only because it was slippery but also for the high escarpments to reach the top. I can tell you, I was happy to carry only a day pack.

We stopped at the top of the Euro Ridge for a delicious, fresh vegetable lunch while admiring The Alice Valley and the impressive MacDonnell Ranges, before going downhill to Wallaby Gap. I saw a grey wallaby standing behind a hill. I took my camera out and lucky me; I was able to photograph it. Grey wallabies are difficult to see, as they are very shy. After arriving at our destination, we were driven to our campsite.

Each one of us was allocated a personal tent, and a personal swag for the full length of the trek, with our private code on each pack. What is the meaning of 'swag' in Australia? It is a canvas with high density foam mattress, including a pillow and a canvas flap that goes over our head. We were told to choose our own pitching spot. All the members were actively putting their tents up, while I was scratching my head looking at the different parts of the tent that I had scattered in front of me. I wished I could have a magic wand with me. I did not know what to do. I had being camping only one single day when I was a 26 year old, two days with my daughter, Sabine and her family at 60, one night at Orisson in France at 64, when I climbed the Pyrenees, and the tents were already set up.

Poor me, I was in big trouble. I had noticed climbing into the 4WD, in Alice Springs, that the other members of the group looked like seasoned walkers and campers.

'Well, Claude be brave and see what you can do'.

Needless to say I had made a mess of it, when one member, George, who had already finished pitching his tent, realised that nothing much had happened in my corner and realised that I was in trouble, but was too shy to ask for help. George kindly decided to show me how to erect the tent and asked me if I had ever put one up. Obviously, I had to tell him the truth and replied to his surprise: 'never' and he started to laugh. His reaction said it all.

Can you imagine: reaching the age of 70 and not knowing how to pitch a tent? Well, I have to say, my life has been quite different than most.

A group meeting was planned at a specific time, and without George's help, I think I would still be trying to put my tent up. Let me assure you that well before the end of our trip I had become an expert, even in the rain!

Rose and Archer informed us of our daily routine which would be: early starts, big breakfast with freshly brewed coffee or tea before packing up, dismantling the tent, and at a precise time we were to start walking, stopping for lunch. At the end of the day when we arrived at our campsite, we would pitch our tent, at most places, have an evening meal together, and meet and talk about the next day's walk, we would shower only at some places, and so wipes were quite necessary. There was no thought about washing our clothes. At the campsite, the composting toilets were placed at an area by our guides. What is a composting toilet? It is to say a simple bucket, though you can't wee in it: a real challenge for any female walker! You have to cover your excrement with some sand or sawdust, as another member needs to use the composting toilet.

I may say: very ecological. Water being so precious, we were allowed one litre of water per person to wash ourselves. To wash our hands a small plastic bottle was hung on the branch of a bush or tree leaving a trickle of water passing through. The dirty water was collected in a container to be recycled later on, somewhere else. We had plenty of drinking water.

On clear nights, away from the 'lights pollution' of our cities, I could lie down and enjoy the beauty of millions of stars above my head. I could not believe that I was in the middle of Australia and walking on this ancient trail which was known to be unrelentingly rocky and hard under foot. The temperatures between the nights and the days were extreme, beanies and gloves were worn, as well as warm jackets.

After a good night's sleep, a big breakfast was waiting for us. Then we had to dismantle our tent, put our swag and belongings the fastest possible way back into the 4WD, and go back on the trail.

Rose and Archer were amazingly great cooks and we always had fresh vegetables. The company catered very well for vegans and vegetarians, a big plus, as there were no shops around.

On day two, the weather was not at its best. It was overcast, and we walked in some rain. I was stopping all the time, as I wanted to photograph everything I could see. It is quite comprehensible at my age; I may not have the chance to walk it again. Unfortunately, the rain entered into my camera and it 'died' on me. It was the one I had used crossing France and Spain. I was very devastated, that is the least I can say. It was a present from two friends. However, Rose told me not to worry, she would lend me hers. Needless to say, I was very grateful and light hearted as I started walking again.

The path was rugged and took us to Scorpion Pools and through woodlands. I could not believe it, in front of me, there were so many wild flowers. A few days earlier, this area, which is on the edge of the most deserted area of Australia, had received some rain and all the bushes were in bloom. We climbed up Hat Hill Saddle, where we could see the rugged Chewing's Ranges. What! Did I hear correctly? Rugged! Well, what have I climbed up to now? This section had nearly killed me! We ended our second day at Simpsons Gap.

The next morning, we started before daylight, as we had a long day ahead about 25 kilometres, and only

God knows the conditions of the trail. The colour of the landscape was out of this world; the grass was knee-high with flowers of incredible colours such as yellow, rose, blue, and white. It was a long walk following low ridges and hills, to the beautiful gorges of Bond and Spring Gap made of granitic gneiss formed around 2,000 million years ago, with their red colour. I was the last one to arrive at the campsite, but I had made it. I experienced such a pleasure looking at the scenery of this amazing part of Australia. I wanted to absorb everything. Nature has given us so much. We finished at Jay Creek.

During the nightly meeting, we were informed that the next four days were the most beautiful ones, with spectacular scenery but very rugged, maybe the most rugged in the world. My heart sank! On our itinerary, all the sections were noted: - medium – hard – very hard. This one was noted 'hard' section.

In the morning, we left Jay Creek for Standley Chasm under a sky of red colours and some clouds. At first, we followed the river bed of Jay Creek. It is very scenic with red cliffs and large gum trees. The trail follows high level steep climbs, the most challenging on the Larapinta Trail. It was hard, I may say:

yes, very, very hard for me. It rained, at times, which made the walk more difficult. We had to climb up and down rocky slopes and boulders, and followed rocky stream beds, high magnificent quartzite ridges, high saddles, many rock faces and gorges. Yes, this was a very rugged section.

I had gone down steep climbs with unstable stones. At times, I had to scramble down rock faces. I was doing it the same way I had climbed down along my first Camino from Vezelay, Northern Central France, maybe not technically safe, but so what? Seeing Archer's look at the way I was descending the cliff, I thought I was going to give to him a heart attack. On the Saint James' Way in France, I was walking alone and as I had never trekked, no one could see if I was descending correctly or not. I had learnt to get over my fear of heights and every time, I always made it in one piece. I felt very proud of myself and eventually, I had learnt to embrace the challenges. Along that section of the Larapinta Trail, I had the same feeling as I was completely outside my comfort zone. For me, the important thing was that I arrived safely at the bottom of the mountain.

The view at the top of Loretta's Lookout, which is the highest point on Chewing's Range, is absolutely impressive and spectacular with 360 degree views.

We followed a rugged section, with high ridges, rock faces and high saddles. I arrived last again. Archer was always keeping a watchful eye over me. We finished the day at Standley Chasm, which is a popular tourist site. We were camping at a private place. All the tents were erected. Can you imagine my joy! I did not have to pitch my tent, I felt so fortunate, and a few minutes later the rain welcomed us again.

There was a special event, that evening, an Arrernte woman was coming to talk to us about her cultural traditions. I was so looking forward to it. I wanted to learn so much about the aboriginal traditions. When I saw her, I knew we had to meet for whatever reason. I approached her and we started a conversation, till Rose came and interrupted us, but we had time to exchange our mobile numbers, so we could meet again in Alice Springs. I was on top of the world!

The Arrernte aboriginal woman shared with us her culture and we were able to gain insight into the oldest living and continuous cultures in the world. Their ways, as a society, are quite complex to understand, in comparison to our European culture though I could see some similarities: dialect, and caring for the land, as we used to do in the 'old continent'. Things that I had learnt as a child when I was staying on a farm, as after the war my parents had to work and could not look after me, and as well, my father's love for the land.

Unfortunately, since the Industrial Revolutions, many of us have lost our connections to, and respect for the land, as greed is our modern motto, though there is a revival on very many different levels. It is something Aborigines and Indigenous people of many countries have not lost and we should learn again from them. Even more so nowadays, as every day we are talking about climate change and its consequences.

The history of the Indigenous Australians, the oldest surviving race, has been recorded as going back 65,000 years ago. They were semi-nomadic, and followed the seasonal food sources. There was only a limited range of food and the women, with their knowledge, knew exactly where to dig to find food and water. The Indigenous Australians were also hunter-gatherers and used to trade between tribes.

Many communities have a very complex kinship structure and very strict rules about marriage. In Central Australia, in traditional societies, the men are required to marry women of a specific moiety (kinship). During the annual gathering called 'corroborees', goods were traded and exchanged, and marriages were arranged amid appropriate ceremonies, as the semi-nomadic groups were small, and in doing so, inbreeding was impossible. Their values and beliefs enable them a sense of identity and meaning, social relationship and extended family. This correlates with Europe as arranged marriages were quite common and each area spoke their own dialect.

My question is? Are we not connecting with each other at a deeper level when one speaks our own language: be it tribal, family, and country that we were born into? To me, language creates us, it is where we belong, and it shows who we are. How many years does it take to learn another language? Language makes our heart sing, we are connecting, understanding each other to the deepest part of our soul thanks to the finesse of the language of someone or of a nation. As French born, I knew that over the years, in fact since 1546, very gradually, the French language took over all the dialects or 'patois' spoken all around France. Nowadays, there is a renaissance in the 'patois'.

Some regions have kept their dialects and you can still hear the Occitan, Corsican, Breton, Basque and others.

For the Australian Indigenous people, the Dreamtime is extremely important, as it describes the Aboriginal spiritual beliefs and their existence. That is to say, at the very beginning of creation. Their people's spirits created the universe, humans and animals, plants, skies, water, and the weather. They have a deep spiritual connection with the land and its people, their environment. We can see this through the Aboriginal Australian art made by Indigenous people which includes painting, painting on leaves, wood and rock carving as well as sculpture. The Aborigines practise their secret ceremonies in areas or mountains where genders do not mix, for example: Uluru is a secret mountain for the men and Kata Tjuta for women.

After the talk and our evening meal, we said good bye to the Arrernte Aboriginal woman, and thanked her. She left me and I presumed it was the same for the other members, with a lot of food for thought. I found some resemblances with our Westerner's culture. The Aboriginal people believe that a super being or an entity has created plants, animals, man and woman, so they could procreate and enjoy the land. The land in the Centre of Australia was not kind to them, but they learnt how to survive and respect the land, which, in a sort a way, became their Master. I saw carved posts and objects.

What about us? The Christian Faiths believe in one God, or source. God has created plants, animals, man and woman so pro-creation could happen. We had a pagan culture before Christianity. In Europe, most ancient churches were built above pagan temples, and we can see their work of art on the columns left in the churches. The churches were built above or close to running springs or brooks as water was respected. It was thought that running water was purifying the soul, in a way, taking away all our sins. I was looking forward to our next meeting in Alice Springs and went to my tent where a camp bed was waiting for me. I thought I would sleep like a baby. Well, that was not the case as I found the camp bed very uncomfortable.

The next morning, we started walking, on a cool morning, at 5.30am, with our companion: the rain.

Though tired, I was ready for the 'very hard' section as it was written in our itinerary. Rose had given me her camera: I was elated.

Even through the mist, I could see the gigantic ochre and orange quartzite peaks surrounding us. After a rough trail we followed a straight valley. It was hard walking on this very rocky path through knolls, and low and high saddles. After a while, I could not see anyone in front of me. As usual, I was the last one on the trail, but, as usual, this did not worry me at all.

I thought: 'You walk at your own pace and all will be well'. There is no rush. On the trekking Company pamphlet, it was written: 'We don't race from A to B'. I wanted to enjoy the colours and discover all my eyes could see, to engrave this amazing landscape forever in my mind, and as well, taking more photos. I wanted to embrace the moment to the fullest.

To reach Brinkley Bluff, one of the highest points along the Larapinta Trail, we followed a long, narrow, jagged ridge. The panorama must be breathtaking but I could only imagine it, as it was still misty when we arrived at the top. From the summit of Brinkley Bluff, the trail descends very steeply and it is a long descent to Rocky Cliff. Archer was worried about me, being so far behind the others. He advised the other members to go forward to the camp, while Archer stayed with me and at times, helped me to climb down some difficult sections. After another saddle, we reached Stuart Pass, which is a sort of easy section after the rough terrain; we had hiked the whole day.

I was last arriving at the campsite. This was no surprise, and I noticed that the other members of the group who had arrived earlier, had put up my tent. I thanked them. What a beautiful gesture of kindness!

After cleaning up, Rose came up to me and to my surprise said: 'Claude, you will not walk tomorrow'. I was flabbergasted as I had arrived at the camp safe and sound. Yes, I was slower than the others: so what? I arrived in one piece. I could not believe it. The reason given to me was: 'we have to take in consideration all the other walkers'.

I was feeling absolutely devastated inside myself, but I had to conform to the decision taken. As every previous night, we met and one of the guides talked about the difficulty of walking the next day. With a heavy heart, I listened to it; once the talk was over I told the other members that a decision had been made for me: 'I will not walk with you tomorrow'.

As I was saying that, tears flowed down my cheeks, I got up and left.

Why did I not confront Rose? The decision was irreversible, I should not question it, I would have to bow and accept it. So be it. The little Claude visualised herself, at the age of 4 or 5, crying quietly in the corner of a room, feeling abandoned once more. Now, I was 70!!! When do we really become the person we should be if in a flash we returned to the little child crying inside? I felt so frustrated

Yes, the trail was hard. Yes, I was fearful at times, especially when I was alone climbing big steep climbs or rocks, though I never verbalised it. But, I overcame my fears and kept on walking till the end. I felt good and proud of myself at the end of the day as I had made it. Why? Why? What do I have to learn from this?

Were my reactions coming from my ego or something much deeper? How many times, in my life, had I stayed on the back burner, always listening to what was said to me, accepting any decision taken for me, always staying quiet, always fearful of creating any havoc if I was going to speak up? I was in the Centre of Australia. I had to accept once more, someone else's decision. I was angry with myself as I did not have the courage to question and challenge that decision. During our life, on this earth we are challenged by various things. These challenges do not come by magic. They are placed in front of us so we can go into our inner self. They are opportunities for us to pull out whatever we need to face up to, and if we are a willing participant, we can find freedom, grow and move forward.

After another non restful night, I put my frustration aside, and I got up for breakfast, I said good bye to the other members, wishing them a wonderful day. In the 4WD, Rose and I arrived at Hugh Gorge. The campsite was set in an amazing place, absolutely divine. I went to help Rose to get all the equipment out of the 4WD. Since the beginning of the trek, I never had the opportunity to wash my clothes. I used wipes to clean my body, having only one litre of water per person to wash ourselves. I was very mindful not to use too much of the litre I was allocated. There was some water in the gorge and I decided to wash my clothes. Afterwards I decided to wander by myself in this incredible environment.

I had to go and walk to heal the inner-child, as all the difficult times in my life had reappeared in a flash and instead of just some frustration I was engulfed by it I had to find compassion for the person who had made the decision, otherwise, the 'free' Claude, I had re-discovered during my first Camino, would evaporate into the ether in no time and I did not want this outcome. I had learnt, I had grown, and a new Claude had surfaced and it should remain as such.

I knew what I had to do, to let go, but still walking slowly and thinking about Rose's decision was not an easy task. I had to release, in this peaceful environment, my frustration. All the logical words, feelings were there, but my mind had to learn to free itself. I should not let it poison my whole being. My body had limitations but not my mind. I should not let my mind take over the feeling that I was not good enough, or I could not achieve this or that. I had to let go of this perception. I had to make a choice, a simple choice, in fact. Did I want to release the pain or nourish the pain by adding more to my sadness for what I had to go through in the different stages of my life?

As I was walking, thinking, releasing my mind, and heart, I started to feel such an enormous energy all around me. It was so powerful, that I could barely breathe. I felt enveloped by an incredible sense of love. In a flash, I understood why I should not have walked with the group that day. Rose was only the instrument: it was for me to feel the love and my connection with this land without anyone around me away from the group.

I let myself be cuddled by such a magical sensation and kept on walking alone, looking, absorbing this magical feeling which kept enveloping me. My thoughts of forgiveness amplified in my soul, and I felt the arms of my father around me, hoping the doggedness that he had shown during his lifetime would help me to pull through till the end of the trek. I kept on walking in this environment which had healed my sadness so quickly. I took time to enjoy all the beauty of this area covered by so many flowers in bloom with their magnificent colours of pink and yellow on the bushes, like if they were giving me so much love without any restrictions. Nature was such a healer and with peace in my heart, I returned, slowly, to the camp and went to my tent as I did not want to lose this wonderful experience. I was full of gratitude for what I had received on that day. This day turned out to be a real blessing.

Eventually, the members of the group arrived, tired but happy with their day's walk. The nights were getting colder and colder and we ate around a campfire. Beanies, gloves, anorak were worn by all the members of the group as we had our evening dinner around the campfire.

The next morning, we left early towards Rocky Gully. We climbed through the Spencer Gorge, and broad creeks, along narrow passages of ochre walls. For a while, the rolling landscape was more arid and the vegetation was not as dense as it was not protected by rocks or trees. We had to climb more rugged, steep and very rocky paths to reach the top of Razorback Ridge: its name says it all. From there, the view was awesome. The trail along the climb down from Hugh View was not as steep, a bit gentler, but challenging, just the same.

On that day, for the first time, since the beginning of the walk, eight days ago, we met some trekkers. Later on we stopped for a break at a rest area, and a few young men, in their late teens or early twenties were already there, reminiscing and complaining about how difficult the trail was, rubbing their feet and wondering what the hell they were doing there. I can tell you, I did connect with them. No words were needed. They had started from Redbank Gorge, walking from West to East as some walkers do. We had started from Telegraph Station, walking East to West.

After a little break, we kept on walking. At times, I walked with George, a member of the group, who kindly shared his coffee, but I walked mostly alone. As usual, I was the last one to arrive at Rocky Gully camp. I had made it. I was happy.

Up at 5.30am the next morning, after we had packed all our gear, we left the camp for Ellery Creek. We kept on crossing the Alice Valley, its sparse vegetation allowed us to have good views in all directions. We got closer to the long and high ridge of the Heavitree Range and many more ridges leaving behind us Chewing's Range. The slopes were rocky, with loose stones. It was a gruelling and insane track with so many small ascents and descents. My feet were scrambling when I was climbing down because of the unstable stones and in a flash I forgot the beautiful experience I had two days ago when I walked alone, close to Hugh Gorge campsite wondering why I had to walk this trail and what led me to it. My thoughts went to my father who, during his compulsory military service had to walk, across the dry parts of the Southern Alps in France. Maybe, he too would have felt the same at some points. The colours of the rocks were white, black, purple and orange red and the scenery was out of this world. Unfortunately, there was not much time to embrace it.

We crossed an area controlled by the Roulpmaulpma Aboriginal Land Trust, who generously allowed us to cross their land. It is where you could find some common brush tail possums. Sadly, I never saw one. We met some Indigenous rangers.

At one stage, we had to walk along a mountain through such a narrow path. I felt very uncomfortable and fear entered me again. I could see myself at the bottom of the cliff quite easily. I had a good look around, standing still, and noticed that I would be able to reach the other side of the mountain by going round it, though it was quite muddy with a steep ascent. I mentioned to Archer my intention of how to reach the other side of the mountain the way I saw it. Archer was not happy for me to do so as this path was slippery and harder. I asked him to trust me. After some deliberation,

Archer must have thought that he had no other choice really, but to trust me. He asked me to leave my backpack with him. I agreed to it heartily. I was relieved not to carry it, and I started to climb up. I do not know how long it took me, but it did not seem to me that long. What was important, I had made it and reached the other side of the mountain in one piece! When I arrived and re-joined the others. Archer said: 'I did not know you were so strong'. His comment was music to my ears.

Due to the terrain, the Larapinta trail did not give me time for personal reflections when I was trekking. I was so concerned about being the last one and every bit of my concentration went where I was putting my feet and I was conscious of the wary eyes from everyone. I sensed their judgement and felt more isolated. Well, I thought: 'You did not walk yesterday. You must be the out-cast'. I shrugged my shoulders, laughed at myself, kept on walking but I never minded stopping and taking a lot of photos.

At sunset, nature was at its best, and showed us some of the awesome colours you can only find in the outback. The sky was looking like it was on fire.

In front of such a beauty, my physical pain would leave me as by magic.

As we arrived at the camp, I was pitching my tent and getting organised for the night when I was asked by Rose and Archer, our guides, to come and see them. I was told, in two days' time, we will reach a very hard section and was informed that I was too slow to join the group. What! Again! This time, I was going to rebuke and asked why? My body and mind had acquired more strength and confidence. It was true that I had never walked such a hard trek, and my body had aged and needed to re-adjust to the demand of trekking every day in these very unhospitable conditions. But so what?

As Archer was present, I asked him if he was happy the way I walked that day, if I had improved as I had tried to keep up closer to the team. What did he think of my ability, my endurance? Though replying 'yes' to my tirade, he did not dare look at me; like he was embarrassed and kept on peeling the potatoes for dinner. I felt that maybe the decision was made without his consent and like me, he had to comply. Rose said that she had to take into consideration what the other members of the group were thinking. Ha!

The cat was out of the box... It was not only their decision but as well the complaints from the other members as I was always the last one to arrive. I thought: So what! I shrugged my shoulders and left. I will not walk in two days' time, so be it!

As I was walking back to my tent, I remembered the comment of one of the members: 'come on Claude, I am cold, hurry, we had to wait for you' – I had never replied back though I felt like rebuking and saying: 'Don't you have a jacket in your backpack. You could put it on. We started at the crack of dawn every morning; we all wore a warm jacket'. But I refrained myself, and smiled saying nothing. Some had confided that this long trek was a 'killer to their ankles'. Back in my tent, I got ready for the next day; Serpentine Gorge to Serpentine Chalet graded 'Hard' on our pamphlet. It was going to take seven hours to cover 15 kilometres.

A long climb leads us to the crest of the Heavitree Range, with 'sweeping' views of the surrounding plains and ridges. Though, saddened by the decisions taken for me the night before, I wanted to enjoy every second of the walk. At times, I was at the front and at other times I was at the back, I did not care a bit.

I noticed some of the members were getting tired and were walking slower. Catherine said: 'Claude, it is not an easy section and you are walking faster than me, wow'. I smiled and thanked Catherine for her kind words, not sharing what I knew. She told me as well that some members of the group were not very kind in their comments about me, as I was walking slower than them. Was I surprised? No, as I remembered Rose's words. We kept on walking the two of us and reached Counts Point with fantastic views to the valley. We crossed rocky ridges till we saw a signpost which lead us to Serpentine Chalet, our campsite.

The group walked to see the ruins of the Serpentine Chalet Dam, I stayed put. I was amazed that a dam, not a big one mind you, was built in such a remote area and I enquired about it. This dam was built in 1958 or early 1960 to attract tourism to this part of the world. The Alice Springs tourism bureau and the pioneer company, Ansett, wanted to bring tourism to this area, but the lack of water and the difficult trail brought it to its demise. Nowadays, you can see the remains such as the concrete slab and other floor foundations. The group re-joined me and we went to our campsite.

Rose, maybe, remembering my questioning about her decision from the previous evening, approached me saying: 'I have noticed your capability but it is not enough and I have decided no matter what, you will not join us tomorrow, as you are, still, too slow in comparison to the others'. I did not reply preferring to keep my feelings to myself.

At daybreak, the group was awakened by the sound of music. It was Archer who, for the first time, had taken his guitar out. Barely awake; I stayed in my swag, where I was nice and warm, while the others left to walk the longest section of the trail. I listened to the songs of the birds and fell back to sleep.

I was feeling so disconnected with the group. Like in every situation there is a positive side, being alone allowed me to focus more and to connect with the spirituality of this ancient trail; the energy was so intense that I wanted to feel it to its fullest. I knew I could do this only when I was alone, without distraction, just me and nature. It was such a feeling of elation. The other members were more interested in talking about football every single day and evening. I was looking for much more. Each one his or her journey!

Later on, I was awakened by Archer playing the guitar and singing. Did he want to soothe my pain, my disconnection with the group and his leader? I did not know. I thanked him and appreciated his kindness.

We packed up and travelled to Ormiston Gorge chit-chatting. At one stage, Archer asked me if I wanted to walk alone to the camping area as it was so easy to find the path. I agreed and at the same time I was hoping to get some connection to the outside world with my phone, I was missing my children and grand-children. Unfortunately, there was no phone connection whatsoever, you have to be with a specific server and I was not.

I recalled my experience at Redbank Gorge, two years ago that led me to walk the Larapinta Trail and my desire to find out. What were the reasons behind it? I had heard these cries, they were heart wrenching, they had overtaken my entire being. Why did I hear these horrible cries? Did I misunderstand the message? What more have I got to learn here? Were these cries coming from the part of me that had not healed yet? Since my early childhood, I have been quite disconnected with others as I was seeing life differently even at a very early age. Not being able to express my feelings, my thoughts, in case I was going to be misunderstood I had become the quiet one, observing, listening to what others had to say, and so often not understanding the way they were analysing different events, but too fearful to be put down if I expressed myself.

I knew that all hardships we have to go through during the course of our life make us stronger human-beings, allowing us to become the person we should become.

As I arrived at the camp, the birds were singing in unison, like if they wanted to heal my heart, but I was more disconnected than ever and still pondering why I was called to walk that trail. It must be something I have to discover. What was it? Eight of my toe-nails were black and blue, soon I would lose them.

As I sat outside my tent, the song of the birds, though quite different from the birds in France, brought me back to my childhood at six or seven years old, where I spent many months at the farm of a distant relative of my father. It was very common in France as at that time there was no kindergarten and both of my parents had to work after the end of World War II. I used to call these relatives 'Pépe' (Grand-dad) and 'Mémé' (Grandma) as they were in their eighties. Their children were living in the other section of the house, with their own young adult children. I was not allowed to go in that part of the house or to visit them. At the farm, there was no child and I was not allowed to mix with any of the children of the village. In those days, there was no television, I do not remember if they had, even, a wireless. My only outing outside of the farm was every Sunday when we went to church on foot or when someone had died as we were visiting the family. I have to say there were not too many dying, but one experience stayed in me forever, and may have led me to understand the meaning of death. In the latter part of my life I became a volunteer in palliative care in a hospital.

At the farm, I used to spend my days helping the adults, the best I could. My chores were to look after the cows, making sure that they did not go outside of their grazing area, or at times removing the stones in the paddocks and helping in the vegetable garden. By removing the stones from the fields, the land could be ploughed without damaging the blades of the tractor too much. During the harvest, there was a sense of community as everyone used to go and help the other farmers. I enjoyed that a lot. With the exception of that brief moment, it was a very lonely time in my life; I was feeling so very lonely and most of all I was missing my Maman, Papa and my sister so much.

Without much distraction, I had developed a way to observe nature, I would stay hours watching nature, scrutinising it, looking at the beauty of a butterfly, a fly, a bee, a snail and at the same time creating a lot of stories in my mind or playing the role of a teacher. I remembered some significant events which would change and affect me forever. I had overheard that a new family had bought the farm next door. I would have been about five or six at that time. The farm was just a few metres across the road, temptation was too great as I could hear a young girl's voice and curiosity took over me; I walked across to the farm, saying nothing to anyone. When I returned the 'grand-father' was so mad at me that he took a section of the bark of a tree and with it smacked me till blood ran down my legs. Trust me, it never happened again. I shared that story with my father when he was in his 90's. He looked at me, smirked; saying nothing, but his eyes said it all: 'well, it was your fault'.

I had very few visits from my parents and for a child a day, a week, a month, or months seemed so very long. Once, I had a visit from my Papa, I was so happy;

I was over the moon, sitting on his lap, I could not stop kissing him, hugging him, till it was time for him to leave. Then, I started crying, screaming would be more appropriate. I was grabbing his clothes as I did not want to let him go. I would scream so much that someone would lift me and carry me to the stable, locking the heavy doors so I could not escape and in doing so, giving my father a chance to leave. I used to scream till I had no tears left in my little body, then I would put myself in a corner of the stable all curled up, feeling so lost and lonely.

From this experience, I became a people pleaser and subservient. I have never been angry with my parents as from an early age; I felt they had no other option and probably, they would have missed me too. I was missing them so much.

My thoughts, here, are not to question, to blame anyone, as maybe, it could have been done in the best of intentions, the environments and thoughts of the time. During our life time, we might make decisions with the best of intentions. However, they can turn out to be so devastating, even centuries later. Over the years, as we have become more in tune with our inner self, or our way to analyse or visualise things, our society has changed, progressed, and can see and analyse differently.

Sitting outside my tent, I looked around me enjoying the beauty of this wild area. Once more, I was so many years later, alone again while I was supposed to walk with a group, how ironic was that! What were the reasons this time? Why was I feeling this way? It was more than just not being fast enough. Was it something much deeper? I needed to find out. I was observing the landscape, taking it all in. When looking with intensity across the stream, I saw on one side of the mountain the carved face of a man so similar to our Aborigines. Was it carved by the wind or what is to show me the truth about the super-natural beliefs of our Aboriginals?

I remembered, two days before, I had seen a heart deeply cut in the mountain by the wind, the rain, or the elements, it was such a similar shape to the one I had seen when I walked around Uluru, carved high up in the mountain, from its position it could not be man-made.

Later on, I was joined by Rose and I asked her, if she had seen this heart-shaped cut in the mountain when we walked between Ellery Creek and Serpentine

Gorge. She looked at me, like if I had said something absolutely out of this world and she replied: 'No'. Rose asked me: where did you see it? I replied: 'maybe next time when you walk that section, take time to look around, and absorb what this land has to offer you'. I knew it was for her a job that led her on this trail, but there was more than just the path.

Needless to say I was stunned! How could she not have noticed it? It was hard for me to believe. She had walked the trail so many times, over the years. I pondered on this and realised that no matter where we are, in full wilderness, in a city, in an office, in a house, we all live in a box, our personal box. We are so controlled by our mind and the busyness of life that we do not see anything else than our own, little personal world. Does that mean we are scared to see outside of the box, scared to see who we are really? Does our mind control us so much, that we are blind to everything around us, except our little personal environment, and habits, till one day, maybe we will "wake up"?

Suddenly, the clouds covered the sky. As I looked up and saw them covering only a section of the sky to form the shape of a heart. I smiled. Was it a message from this ancient land? Was it: 'you are never alone, you might feel alone but you are not we are with you, always. Your freedom is in you, let the others judge you; they don't know your true-self. Let freedom enter your heart and you will live a peaceful life. Embrace all the difficulties coming your way, from them you will learn and grow. Your soul has to be open to all. We are with you, free your soul of misgivings, burn off these residues and walk freely along the path we have created for you'.

The next morning, after a good night's sleep, I re-joined the group and got ready for the day. I had been getting a head-cold for quite a few days, and it had gone down to my chest. My breathing was getting shallower. We started walking a bit later that day, at 8.30am, on a cold and windy morning. No matter what, I was ready for the challenges ahead. This section would take us from Ormiston Gorge to Glen Helen.

Not far from our campsite I met two young Canadian girls from the Rocky Mountains, who were working in Canberra. They were walking and camping on the trail, and they were celebrating Anna's 40th birthday. I stopped to have a chat. I was looking forward to some chin-wagging! I was slow, therefore so what. Prue said:

'We had no idea how hard this trail was going to be' and both of them were questioning their decision. They wanted to do something different to celebrate Anna's birthday. We giggled and I sympathised with them. I chatted a few more minutes, and left not without giving them a hug. I had to catch up with the group and with my reputation; I will have to walk faster, and thought: 'More chance for them to complain about me'.

We were leaving the high ranges. The rolling hillocks allowed us to see the surrounding mountain ranges. We walked for at least two kilometres along sand creeks and rivers and on stones only in the dry creek. Though it is hard to walk on stones all the way, I found it easier than walking on the sand.

There were massive Red Gum trees and many varieties of birds and flowers. We climbed many ridges and zig-zag paths till we reached a look-out, providing us with amazing views on the Heavitree Range, Ormiston Gorge and Mount Sonder.

This section was short, 12 kilometres. We arrived at our eco-camp situated at Ormiston Gorge. Large and quite comfortable tents were erected. After trekking and sleeping most nights in a small tent, I found it was a real luxury. Still no phone connection, I just could imagine my children wondering and worrying! 'Here she is walking, enjoying herself and not giving us any news!' We do worry when our children leave our nest, and cheekily, I thought, well, this is the reverse, isn't it, but I was still worried just the same.

From the campsite we were driving to Glen Helen. I was told we could enjoy a nice warm shower. I was so looking forward to it, after being 11 days on the trail. At Glen Helen historic station, the camping ground was full of caravans with many grey nomads; needless to say it was very busy. I must have put my hopes too high as I had the pleasure of having a cold shower. Looking on the bright side of things, I had a shower. The Finke River is close by. I did not go there as two years before after trekking around Uluru, I went and fell on the slimy rocks and hurt my tailbone.

At its origin, Glen Helen was a cattle station. Due to the difficult climate, very little rain or too much of it, the station was abandoned several times. It was re-built, then burnt down and flooded again, till some new owners took the bull by the horns and rebuilt. Now, it welcomes campers and provides comfortable accommodation.

The cold shower did not help my chest problem. As I did not want to say anything, in case I was not allowed to walk again, I decided not to eat around the campfire as the coldness and dampness of the night would have made matters worse. I sat under a tarpaulin and ate by myself.

At dusk, without the modern pollution of electric lights, I kept embracing the beautiful field of stars. In this incredible environment, and before entering my tent for a good night's sleep, I was contemplating and reflecting for a while looking at the carved Aboriginal head on the side of the mountain when I remembered the Chief Dan George's words: 'Wisdom of the Elders'

- May the stars carry your sadness away
- May the flowers fill your heart with beauty
- May hope forever wipe away your tears and above all
- May silence make you strong

After a warm breakfast, we set off in the icy morning to Rocky Bar Gap which was a hard section. I walked in Catherine's company again, who was starting to be very tired. I appreciated our interaction. I shared with her my first walk across France and Spain, which has helped me to release my past and told her that I felt so disconnected with the group.

During our dinner, the members of the group asked me if I believed in God or in a super being. As I replied: 'yes' some lifted their eyes and the subject was closed, before even being opened.

Under the stars, I reflected on their question. People, friends, family will pass through your life. Some briefly, some will leave such a big hole in your heart that you think you will never be able to live anymore as you are dying inside and your light is gone. All challenges we are encountering are here to help us to grow. Through the solitude of the heart we need to learn and grow as well. This is life. It is not easy, but it is the only way for us to become who we should be and be able to help and connect to the fullest if someone shares with us their life and sorrows. Then, only can we become their listening ear with an open heart on a much deeper level. Even with a broken heart we have to keep on walking along our path as God or the Universe wants us to keep on walking so we can grow and grow. We have to learn to accept everything coming our way. There is always a reason for everything. To me, it is very important not to share what was said in full confidence.

The trail was crossing spinifex covered plains and was hard going as the Mac-Donnell Ranges are more broken with high ridges and hills. We climbed many hills with steep ascents that day and reached the top of Hill Top Lookout where we could see all the surrounding area, with Mount Sonder in all its beauty. The descent from Hill Top Lookout was stony, and challenging, I may say.

What are spinifex clumps and Mallee trees? Both originated in Australia, the spinifex grass has coarse spiny stiff of sharp leaves, therefore when you cross an area full of them, wearing gaiters is a plus. Mallee tree is the name given by the Aborigines and from the family of the Eucalyptus.

The next day would be the day when at last, we would reach Redbank Gorge, where I had two years ago, this strange experience which led me to walk the Larapinta Trail at the age of 70. Will I find the answer to my questions? I wanted to touch the cliff again. I had so many questions in my mind.

I slept like a baby, and ready for the challenge ahead, hoping that tomorrow I would have all the answers I was hoping for.

They are many creeks to cross; the clumps of spinifex are everywhere as well as mallee forests. At one stage we passed in front of a conical hill, looking like a Mexican hat.

After the difficulty of the trail since the beginning, this section was quite easy in comparison. We arrived back at our campsite, to my disappointment; we did not pass or go close to the section of the gorge I wanted so much to reach. It was only about two or three kilometres away from the campsite.

The group was tired and did not want to go to Redbank Gorge. I informed Rose and Archer of my intention to walk to the gorge. I started alone and later on Catherine and Archer followed me. I crossed the sandy banks of the Redbank Creek. All along, I could see Red Gums and Ghost Gum trees which were following the water course, and then the path became very rocky, narrower and with scrambling areas. Eventually, I reached the end of the track and its canyon. It had been raining more than usual and the basin was full of water, impassable, to my despair. It was impossible to cross it. I sat for a long time, on the edge of the pool looking across at this majestic orange coloured cliff, unreachable, with a heavy heart.

I was so close and in the same time so far. Saddened, I returned the same way to the campsite. It was not meant to be. As I was walking back I saw a lot of heart-shaped stones, just like I used to see on the Saint James' Way and smiled.

We had our dinner then I went to my tent as the next day we would have to wake up at 2.30am for an early start. At 3.30am, we would trek in the darkness of the night: Mount Sonder, so we could arrive before sun rise at the top and see the birth of a new day. Mount Sonder at 1,380 metres of altitude is the highest peak of the Larapinta trail and fourth highest peak in the Northern Territory. Mount-Sonder and its surrounds are known by the Indigenous as Rwetyepme. It has an important religious significance for the Western Arrernte Indigenous people.

We walked the trail in full darkness, with a head-light. Rose asked me to walk up in front with her. She realised that my head-light was not appropriate and kindly lent me hers while she walked with mine. In the dark of night we could not see anything. One member was grumbling as I was in the front, she was complaining and I heard: 'With her in the front we will never make it on time' I smiled, shrugged my shoulders and kept on climbing as fast as I could. In the end, we arrived on time to see a new day dawning. It was so cold, so very cold, and windy at the top. I was like ice as well as the others. Rose had carried some coffee in a thermos. We all enjoyed a lovely piping hot coffee and later on, a light breakfast.

In the darkness, and on the horizon, slowly, slowly a horizontal red light appeared. Slowly, slowly the red horizon gently disappeared as shone through the sun and showed us its full beauty. Its centre, looking like a huge round ball, filled up with a white-light; and around it another orange coloured one. As the sun rose we saw all its red rays embracing the land and showing us the full 360 degree views to the pleasure of us all. It was magical, really something out of this world and for us all to remember all our life.

From this magnificent viewpoint, I noticed the remote desert peaks, and most of the MacDonnell Ranges and as well most of the sections the group had walked in the last 15 days, 13 days for me, and the Northern Territory's highest point at 1,531 metres as well Gosse Bluff.

We trekked back down on the same path, and to my amazement I discovered what I had climbed up and the condition of the trail. As I ascended it, I crossed path with a father and his little seven year old son, climbing Mount Sonder. This little one was complaining, but never stopped climbing. I was in awe. I congratulated him and gave him a hug. His father smiled and thanked me.

Eventually, we arrived back at the campsite. I felt so blessed to have been the witness of a new day, at the top of Mount Sonder. It was a magical moment. Nature at its best and as always never discriminating, giving, and showing us the way we should live.

The next day would be a short walk to Ormiston Pound Loop. Though not part of Larapinta Trail it is a must-see for anyone visiting this area.

Some sections were nearly flat. We followed ridges and hills, when at one stage; I could see my companions from afar. I was last again; one cannot change, right? Otherwise I would lose my reputation! No way! I laughed and thought: 'At least you have taken many beautiful photos'.

We crossed dry or semi-dry creek beds, with towering cliffs on each side with red-orange vivid colours typical of the outback and along the Larapinta Trail. Ghost

Gum Eucalyptus grows everywhere even half way up the rock walls. Some sections are covered with stones- huge stones, I would say boulders. Arriving at an area on a bank of the river, Archer informed everyone that we had to cross the river. What? We had to cross the river!! OMG! Let me breathe a bit. Archer put his backpack above his head and crossed telling us exactly where we should put our feet, not too much to the right, not too much to the left.

The water was well above his waist. I was thankful to be wearing swimwear. Bravely one by one the group crossed, taking their clothes off, with the bare minimum while I was pondering how I could cross this river without wetting my backpack. Ok. Carry everything above my head including my hiking boots. Well, what if I slip, if I lose my balance? Archer, who had arrived on the other side, could see nothing much was happening where I was standing, and decided to cross the river again and said: 'Ok. Claude. - give me your backpack and follow me, all will be well, put your feet where I put mine'. Nice to say: 'how could I see his feet when they were under the water?'

I could imagine myself at the bottom of the river and everyone laughing. Well surprise, surprise, and to my amazement, I crossed it without any problem. Ha, ha, ha. No one laughed, and I missed the opportunity to be the queen of the pack that day!!!

I went to put my clothes back on, looking for a huge rock to hide behind. Then we started climbing a big escarpment reaching Ghost Gum Look Out, with excellent views of all the different types of layers of the surrounding cliffs.

At lunch time Rose joined us with our meals. Very soon it would all be over. We all sat on the edge of the creek, each of us taking a personal spot, far from each other, not talking. I supposed all were reflecting on their personal journey. In a few hours, we would all depart and return to our hotel then fly back home. Would we keep in touch? Or were they just there for a brief moment in your life? In the 4WD, one member called out to me and said: 'Claude you do not have to say to your family and friends that you have not walked the 16 days'. I looked at her, shocked, stunned, I could not believe it. Why should I lie? I replied 'The truth is the truth, I will not lie'. Was this remark to put her conscience at rest? I did not know, nor cared.

We packed up and walked to the Ormiston Gorge Complex, before visiting the Centre and being driven back to Alice Springs. Catherine and I were dropped off first and said good-bye to everyone.

The next morning, I had an early breakfast with Catherine in the centre of Alice Springs, who reiterated how she was sorry for me, with the comments of the others, because I was slower than everyone else. I told her not to worry; it was all water under the bridge. We departed and hugged.

I was looking forward to my meeting with the Arrernte Aborigine who came to talk to us at Standley Chasm. She had left her executive job with the Australian government to devote herself to her passion: Reconciliation and Closing the Gap Initiatives with all Australians, as well as raising cultural awareness, I admired her courage and determination. I had the pleasure of meeting her family and we shared a meal together. We drove to Anzac Hill which stands high overlooking Alice Springs. I told her reconciliation is the way to go, not only with our Indigenous but with all the different nations. If it is probably not possible for all the nations around the world, at least, with willingness from all parties and love, this can be achieved. Forgiveness, on both sides, is the only way to go and move forward.

Following our conversation she thought that I should read a book called: 'Traditional Healer of Central Australia: Ngangkari' from the Ngaanyatjarra Pitjantjatjatjara Yankunytjatjara (NPY) Women's Council, which had received many awards and took me to a bookstore. To my disappointment all these books had been sold, though an order had been sent, and the bookstore's owner was waiting for its delivery. As we were leaving, a delivery man entered the shop. And yes, inside that box, there was the book: I was blessed once more.

For thousands of years, the Ngangkari have nurtured the physical, emotional and social well-being of their people, and have created a close relationship with health professionals and practitioners of Western Medicine, sharing their natural healing techniques.

We departed and hugged. I was walking back to my hotel when I was approached by an Aboriginal Woman, who asked me for some money for food. Both of us walked to a grocery store. I told her she could buy whatever she needed. I was surprised to see she took mostly sugary drinks, instead of nice, healthy and nourishing produce.

What have we taught them! She was happy, and I was happy too, as she gave me a beautiful smile when we departed.

Around mid-morning, the next day, I decided to go back to Anzac Hill. At the bottom of the hill I had to make a decision either to take the steps and path or the road leading to the top of the climb. I chose the steps and path. I was about half-way up when I came across three young French students. You can imagine their surprise when I approached them and spoke in French to them. They told me that they loved travelling around Australia with its amazing variety of landscapes, and learning about our Indigenous culture. To my surprise, Thierry, one of the students, was born in the same village as my father. Mind you, it was a very small French village when my father was born, and now it is a small town. I felt my father was sending me a 'Clin d'oeil' (a wink).

I arrived back at the hotel when suddenly a hailstorm started and within a few minutes, the balls of ice covered the ground just like snow. I thought about the rain when I started my journey in the Red Centre and now finishing it with the hail. The electricity went off and I went back to my room, lay on my bed looking at the ceiling and pondered. I thought about the new group of walkers who had left the same morning to walk the Larapinta Trail. I hoped that they would be safe.

Why was I called to walk the Larapinta Trail? What have I learnt on this ancient trail? Has the attitude of my fellow walkers helped me to grow, to see life from a different angle, to learn about my limitations, to be more assertive, to be courageous, and give myself a voice? So many questions I could not answer.

Indigenous tribes and many of us believe in the afterlife. What were the desperate cries I heard at Redbank Gorges in 2014? Did I hear them to remember the sorrow of all Indigenous people around the world, the sorrow of the entire world, the sorrows of the ones we have passed as they could see the way we are leading our lives on this earth? Are they the cries about the way the world is leading its way: killing, hurting, abusing, controlling, and destroying in the name of greed? Are we so accustomed to our way of life that some think, it is a normal way to live as we are not touched by these terrible things, and we can't change anything anyway?.

What have we not learnt over the centuries? We might have more knowledge, and that has to be proven, as I think we have lost our wisdom.

Walking on this beautiful ancient land in the centre of Australia, many questions remain. Do we need to change our ways, to stop destroying, to re-create the way nature was with all, its beauty? Otherwise nature will take its revenge and create havoc on this earth. When nature decides to act, we might start to listen and to understand.

Was it to show me, though already I knew, that we need a better society based on love, care, and understanding of others to the best of our ability, so we could have a better world? It was not all about walking; it was much more, as I have felt a deep connection with this land and its inhabitants.

I feel that we have to talk, to walk hands in hands, understand and respect each other tradition and acknowledging the good and the bad done by each side. The healing of each nation can only be resolved by will, understanding and respect.

Anger will bring more anger which will lead to war and separation instead of closeness. If we open our hearts love will bring peace.

The Red Centre is really amazing. My journey was mine, mine alone. I felt blessed to have been able to walk it, see it, and learn from it. It will stay with me forever.

I left the Red Centre, not knowing what the message was, but hoping that one day I will fully understand it. It could have been the cries of the world and maybe the answer to my questions were very simple: Forgiveness and love one another.

If you wish to walk the Larapinta Trail, remember the trail is hard and rocky with sharp quartzite. It is very challenging on your feet and boots. It is wise to have new boots that you have broken down. Choose well; make sure that they fit your feet well. You will need to carry at least three litres even in winter, warm clothes for the cold nights, and a pair of trekking poles. You will find, below the itinerary of the Trail, if you want to walk it. If you decide to do so, I wish you an amazing time!

The Itinerary: 16 Days on the Larapinta Trail

Day	From/To	Distance	Time	Difficulty
1	Telegraph Station – Wallaby Gap	13.5km	6hrs	Medium
2	Wallaby Gap – Simpsons Gap	10.5km	4hrs	Medium
3	Simpsons Gap – Jay Creek	25km	9hrs	Medium
4	Jay Creek – Standley Chasm	13km	8hrs	Hard
5	Standley Chasm – Birthday Waterhole	17km	9hrs	Very Hard
6	Birthday Waterhole – Hugh Gorge	17km	9hrs	Very Hard
7	Hugh Gorge – Rocky Gully	16km	7hrs	Medium
8	Rocky Gully – Ellery Creek	15km	6hrs	Medium

Day	From/To	Distance	Time	Difficulty
9	Ellery Creek – Serpentine Gorge	14km	6hrs	Medium
10	Serpentine Gorge – Serpentine Chalet	15km	7hrs	Medium
11	Serpentine Chalet – Ormiston Gorge	29km	10-12hrs	Hard
12	Ormiston Gorge – Glen Helen	12km	5hrs	Medium
13	Glen Helen – Rocky Bar Gap	15km	7hrs	Hard
14	Rocky Bar Gap – Redbank Gorge	12km	4hrs	Medium
15	Redbank Gorge – Mt Sonder	16km	7hrs	Hard
16	Ormiston Pound Walk	8km	4hrs	Easy

CHAPTER 2

Walking with a group in Nepal

Poon Hill – 3,210 Metres Altitude – Nepal

12 days: Nepal tour/trek -
55 kilometres trekking - Plus tours

6 November 2017 - 17 November 2017
at 71 years of age.

How did it come about? Early in January 2017, while I was at home, I received a phone call from my daughter, Sabine.

'Maman, would you like to trek in Nepal?'

Astounded, I replied:

'What! Trekking in Nepal? No, not at all'

'It has never been on my mind or on my bucket list. Nepal! No way! No way!' I was visualising myself climbing in the Annapurna, and chuckled, after my experience the previous year with the Larapinta

Trail, while my daughter was keeping on talking over the phone.

'Maman, one of my colleagues is going next November; it is a 12 day trek/tour'.

Once my daughter informed me of the cost, it took me only two seconds to tell my daughter:

'Ok, I will do it, book me in'.

Once I hung up, I realized what I had done. This was not unusual for me in my old age, as we are freer from most of our responsibilities, once our children have left the nest. My decision was made; I was going to trek in Nepal, the Poon-hill trek at an altitude of 3,210 metres.

As the penny dropped, I thought:

'Oh Claude, you are still mad! Well, you discovered the real you at the age of 64, when you crossed two countries, France and Spain, alone and on foot; maybe it is a point of no return. By the way, do you realise that you are 71 now and have not trekked many times?'

I laughed and shrugged my shoulders. Closing the door of my home behind me, I went for a walk still stunned by my daring decision.

A few months before going to Nepal, I shared my thoughts with a member of the Brisbane Camino Group, Diana, about my project. As I was talking, Diana became very excited, saying she would like to walk the Poon Hill trail too. I gave her all the information and on 3 November 2017, we met at Brisbane International Airport and flew out to Kathmandu, all excited about this new adventure.

Nepal is in South Asia, a landlock between the Himalayas, the Borders of China in the North and India in the East, South and West.

After more than twelve hours of flying, not including the stoppage time in Singapore, we landed at Tribhuvan-Kathmandu airport at around 10.00pm. As soon as we had passed the Customs, we were hassled by taxi-drivers: it was a real cacophony. We tried to make our way through the crowd and the hasslers, and looked for our taxi, when we saw a man holding a sign, with the name of the Tour Company we had booked. He directed us to a taxi, after a brief 'Hi' from the driver we were transferred to our hotel which was in the Centre of Kathmandu at the Thamel centre. Both of us were relieved. At the reception, the hotel staff were very accommodating and considerate.

After completing all the formalities, we took possession of our individual bedroom.

The next day, we went to an Exchange Money Booth, not far from the hotel and with some local money, we started discovering Kathmandu. Most of the streets were decorated with prayer flags, and there were people everywhere. Cars and motorcycles were going in all directions and sharing the streets with pedestrians. There was no order, but no one was shouting, yelling, bullying, it was full harmony. What amazed me the most was there did not appear to be any accidents occurring. I saw a few pedestrian crossings, but no one was using them. There were potholes everywhere. I did not see anyone falling down or tripping on them. There was such busyness, so many people. I noticed that everyone was smiling, relaxed: it seemed so normal to them. It was my first day in Nepal and I was learning my first big lesson, as for us Westerners we want everything perfect and we complain about any little thing which annoys us. I was wondering what would happen if I decided to drive on the wrong side of the road back in Australia, or in any countries in the Western world. I could picture the scene and I started laughing.

After a good night's sleep, we went for breakfast, and met two Americans from California, Lee and Jim, and a French couple, Pierre and Isabelle, from Grenoble, a city not far from where I was born. Pierre and Isabelle were returning to France after their trek to Base Camp. Jim and Lee, who had been here for a little while, asked us if they could show us Kathmandu and come with them to the Monkey Temple, Swayambhunath. We accepted with eagerness.

As we crossed the city on foot, I was still challenged by the confusion in the streets, but mostly by the dirt and the many potholes. Some sections of the main streets were like dirt roads we would find in some areas in the Outback of Australia, as so many trucks, tut-tuts, and motorcycles were travelling on the unsealed streets. The Nepalese people were wearing masks to protect their lungs. The unsealed roads were creating a lot of dust. Diana decided to buy one, but I did not. Then, as we walked along the streets, we saw a cow lying in the middle of the road. No one was disturbing her, but to my horror, hundreds of electric wires were hanging on a wooden pole without any protection: there was no security whatsoever. How could the electricians find the proper wires for individual houses or shops? What if a wire fell on the ground? How many people could be electrocuted? My Western mind was mystified. It was mind boggling. Many years ago, while walking the Saint James' Way, I had lived the simplest life possible with all my possessions in my backpack, sleeping in dormitories, and living my every day walk, with very little as I was staying in the cheapest places, but what I was seeing now was so different. I had discovered that man, like a chameleon, can adapt to any situation he is faced with during his lifetime.

On each side of the road, the shops with their deep red, orange, and blue painted doors were brightening the streets. The contrast was incredible. The shops were small, like 'bric a brac' stores, displaying whatever tourists might want to bring back home. Owners or salespersons were sitting on the stairs, leading to their shop, waiting for prospective buyers. We stopped at one shop and I bought a Mala Bead Necklace.

As we were walking across the city I saw more devastation. In a little area, where probably a small house would have stood, stones and bricks were scattered everywhere, as well as plastic bags, and many other types of rubbish.

In the middle of this garbage, a goat was scavenging, eating whatever grass had grown between the bricks in the middle of this small area.

My thoughts went to what Nepal had to endure, since April 2014, and the many challenges the Nepalese had to overcome. Indeed, in mid-April 2014, an avalanche on Mount Everest killed 16 Sherpas and the same year at the beginning of August, a landslide killed 156 people. In late August, floods killed 102 people, and then a freak snowstorm in the Annapurna Region in October killed several dozen trekkers. I should not forget the worst catastrophe affecting Nepal on 25 April 2015. There was an earthquake of magnitude 7.8 and numerous aftershocks causing death and destruction.

Thousands died and thousands were injured. The earthquake triggered avalanches on Mount Everest killing more people. Damage to the buildings and infrastructure was widespread; many historical monuments including the UNESCO World Heritages sites listed Kathmandu Valley. There was still so much to do to bring the city back to what it was prior to the catastrophic quake.

Walking along the streets, I saw some black Hindu statuettes. Some grains of cooked rice were scattered on them as offerings, as well as beautiful marigold flowers.

Suddenly, from afar, there appeared behind the buildings the top section of a white shining dome. On the top it looked like a gold pointy hat and two huge eyes. It was the Monkey Temple's Stupa, which is a commemorative monument of Buddhist Shrine.

Crossing a bridge over a river, I saw, to my horror that the river was much polluted; both banks were covered with rubbish, plastic bags, and broken polystyrene boxes, with children playing in the middle of them. My heart sank.

Eventually, we arrived at the base of the Monkey Temple, where the monkeys are kings. At the bottom of stairs, the statues of Buddha and lions were guarding the entrance. To reach the Monkey Temple, we had to climb 365 steep stone steps. Jim told us to hide our drinking bottles as the Monkeys would come and grab them from us. The monkeys had learnt how to open plastic drinking bottles so they could drink whatever was left in them. I observed them and was so surprised by their agility and intelligence.

They were so quick in grabbing your bottle that you did not have time to react and you could not fight with them. As we climbed we could see a panoramic view of Kathmandu, and how spread out the town was, as well as a breathtaking view of the Himalaya ranges.

After some huffing and puffing we reached the top. It was buzzing everywhere: Westerners, Nepalese, Indian and Chinese. The Nepalese and Indian women were wearing their beautiful, colourful saris. A young Nepalese couple approached me wanting to take a photo with me. I agreed, touched by their kindness and thought: 'It must be my grey hair'. I have to say, I did not see any other grey haired person climbing the 365 stairs. Due to our different languages we could not converse, and so we smiled acknowledging each other. It was all so simple, so natural, just a simple sense of belonging as human beings on this planet.

The Monkey Temple or Swayambhunath is the oldest and holiest Buddhist temple in Nepal, dating from 460 A.D. Legend says that it was born out of a lotus flower and stood as a hallmark of faith and harmony. It offers peace, freedom, joy to everyone and helps us to achieve perfect enlightenment.

A Stupa is a commemorative Nepalese monument or temple. This one was made of four equal sites. His eyes were painted on the four corners of the Stupa. I was intrigued by his eyes as they seemed to follow me in the four directions of the Stupa as if the eyes of the Buddha were looking at me inquisitively, trying to reach the deepest part of my soul. It was a very strange sensation.

We visited a small temple, called Shantipur (place of peace). I did not feel peaceful in there. It felt mysterious, and somewhat uncomfortable.

At the bottom of a staircase there was a brightly painted door. Curiosity took over and we opened it to find a huge, three metre high Tibetan prayer wheel, and around the door a dozen smaller wheels that you can spin very easily, which I did.

You will find many various shrines, Hindu temples and replicas of deities, as well as many small shops. We wandered everywhere I was trying to grasp and absorb it all, to the best of my ability. All good things have to end, and it was time to return. Climbing down the stairs, as you can guess, was so much easier!

On our way back we stopped at Nirvana café, the staff and the owners were so accommodating, always smiling, their kindness and gentleness was incredible. From the top of the roof café we had amazing views of the mountain ranges. Many frames were hanging everywhere; on one of them the name 'Nepal' was decomposed, with an English word beside each letter and on another frame was written the basic expressions in Nepalese, translated into English.

I like the meaning of the word NEPAL:

>N – NEVER
>E – END
>P – PEACE
>A – AND
>L – LOVE

Reading this, I connected with Nepal. I was touched by this translation. Yes, our world needs so much "Peace" and "Love". Every human being wants peace but really what are we doing about it? Is our world not full of anger, wars, and ego?

After we left the Nirvana Café, we walked in amazement in the city. It was the end of the school day with all the students coming out, when one little girl ran towards me, saying 'Namaste', putting her arms around me. I lifted her in my arms then suddenly out of nowhere a group of school girls surrounded me and asked me for more and more and more hugs. I was holding two or three at the same time, hugging them. They were so happy, so warm, jumping and singing in unison 'Namaste – Namaste'. They were not scared of a foreigner. The spontaneity of these children was heart-warming. It was a magical moment, something to cherish in my heart forever.

Diana, Jim and Lee, who had stopped at a store, caught up with me and we went back to our hotel, along the busy streets. My Western judgment was disappearing bit by bit, leaving a more loving, caring and not so judgmental mind. It felt as if I no longer saw the chaos, the potholes, and the dust. At that moment, I was on cloud nine.

At 11.30pm (23:30), I was awakened by my daughter's co-worker. June was ringing from the front desk her voice sounded so worried. I thought something had happened to her. That was not the case; she was concerned. At the hotel's reception, the staff wanted to take her passport and photocopy it. June was not willing to do so in an unfamiliar country as the receptionist did not give her a proper explanation or would not reply to her questions and concern. It could have been a communication problem. She was overwhelmed and asked the staff to call me. I tried to pacify her and she said: 'And Claude, the airport is worse than Mongolia!' I told her to calm down that all would be well. Awakened, I could not go back to sleep and started writing.

The next morning, we had breakfast with some other guests staying at the hotel and our two new American friends. Later on, we met a young English couple, Chandhi and Divvesh, who were going to trek to Base Camp.

Diana, June and I left the hotel and went to discover a bit more of Kathmandu. There were a lot of Europeans and Americans in the streets. You could hear a multitude of languages coming from everywhere. The dust was so bad that June and I decided to buy a mask and we became 'The Three Musketeers'.

In the evening, we met the other members of the group, Paul and Nola from New Zealand, Juliet from Tasmania, Helen from Brisbane, and our Tour Manager Arjun.

We were told that the following morning we would be picked up to visit Kathmandu, and the Monkey Temple.

'What! The Monkey Temple!'

I asked if we were going to climb the 365 steps. Arjun smiled and replied: 'No, there is a road at the back leading to the top of the hill to the Monkey Temple'. Hearing that I started to laugh: there was a back door!

After breakfast, we were driven to the Monkey Temple. As we arrived at the top, I approached our guide for the day and asked:

'How long will it take for the group to visit the Temple?'

'One and a half hours'

'Well, could I ask a favour? I have already visited the Monkey Temple, yesterday, could I walk about and re-join the group in one and half hours?'

'Ok, but be back on time' was his reply.

'I will, I promise.'

I informed Diana, and she decided to join me.

As we were walking, I noticed a long red building behind a tall heavy metal door. There was a gap and saw many feet with sandals walking up and down. Curiosity overtook me. For some odd reason, I felt the need to discover what was behind this door. I knocked and pushed the gates, finding myself in front of a few monks, books in hands, probably praying. I apologised and walked back. I was stopped by an older monk, who invited me to come in. I waved at Diana who was observing the scene, to come in.

We were allowed to visit the temple; the main room was divided into many sections visible from all corners. Colourful curtains were hanging everywhere. The ceilings were covered, at regular distances, with integrated designs. Even with the busyness of the painting, draping, and shelves full of lions, I felt embraced by such a powerful sense of calmness and peace. What is this sense of peace that took over Diana and I? I do not know but we felt we had to sit down and started praying. A few minutes later, one of the older monks came accompanied by a smiling young monk and introduced us to Prakashik. Prakashik could speak English, such a blessing; his face was so serene and he showed us around. One section was dedicated to the present Dali Lama with a photo of a younger Dali Lama, there was a study room and a prayer room, all painted in bright red, orange, blue and green.

As Prakashik was showing us around we arrived in a courtyard; I informed Prakashik that I had noticed the day before a white building at the top of a mountain and asked if it was by any chance a temple:

'Yes, was his answer, I could take you, there, tomorrow, if you want'.

Sadly, we were leaving for Pokhara, the next day.

'No worries, here is my phone number and when you are back in Kathmandu, just call me, and I will take you up there'.

I thanked him, so humbled by his kindness. After a few photos with the other monks in the court yard, we left. It was time to return and find our group, elated with the meeting we just had and this incredible opportunity.

We re-joined the other members of the group who were enchanted by their Monkey Temple visit and were driven to the Pashupatinah Temple accompanied by a new young female guide, Johanna.

We were driven to Patan Dubar Square and visited the Pashupatinah Temple, which is UNESCO World Heritages listed and was built during the 5th Century and is the most venerated Hindu and Buddhist monument in Nepal. The roof of this two storey temple is in gold copper and, its spire in gold. Around this impressive monument you will find 518 temples. The style of the temple is like a Nepalese pagoda style of cubic construction with amazing and intricate carved wooden rafters that have been hammered and chiselled by the artists. The small and big sculptures are made of clay, stone, metal and wood representing mostly gods, goddesses, animals and birds based on Hinduism and Buddhist philosophies.

Here you will find a two level impressive monument in a fortified courtyard. Its four main doors are made of silver and guarded by Nepalese policemen.

We crossed paths with many nationalities and there are many homeless women and men waiting for us to give them a few rupees. It was the beginning of November, autumn in the Northern Hemisphere, and they were wearing hardly any clothes.

The other attraction of the day was to see the new living goddess; we were on our way to her palace when thousands of hungry pigeons flew over our heads, some landing on the top of the roofs of the various shrines.

Every day at the same time, the young living goddess or Kumari appears from a window in her palace. It is a centuries old tradition. The female child has to be between two and four years old and is chosen from the Newar community, which is the Indigenous to the Kathmandu Valley. The Kumari is chosen by strict criteria: an unblemished body, a chest like a lion and thighs like a deer and eyelashes like a cow, as well as an astrological chart supportive of the King of Nepal. The Kumari is taken away from her parents till she reaches puberty when she is given back to her family. She is allowed to go out only thirteen times a year for special celebrations, wearing very elaborate make-up. She is not allowed to walk outside or touch the ground. It is believed that she is the re-incarnation of a goddess Taleju symbolizing power and protection. It is said that she will bring luck to anyone who lays eyes on her

We arrived in front of the palace and patiently waited for the new goddess to appear. Her name was Trishina Shakya, 3 years old, and had been anointed a few days earlier after replacing the other goddess who could not be goddess anymore as she had reached puberty. Soon, the cobbled stone square in front of the palace was packed with hundreds of worshippers waiting for the new Kumari. Eventually, she appeared at the window with the help of her Hindu carers. Her face had elaborate make-up, her hair was in a tight top-knot and she was wearing a traditional costume. She looked so small, presumably, wondering why all these people were looking at her and maybe frightened by the huge noise of admiration coming from the square. My mother's heart went out to her. It was her first appearance and lasted only a few minutes, maybe too long for her.

We left the square to go and visit a famous and sacred Hindu Temple called Pashupati, on the banks of the Bagmati River. It is a holy place where the dead bodies are cremated and to my surprise, I discovered that there are two sections one at the top for the rich and one at the bottom for the not so rich. It is believed that if the dead are cremated at this place, they will be reborn from a human womb and be a human again and not an animal.

As we entered this holy place we saw a lot of Hindus, their faces covered with coloured powder, which looked like paint. They are called Sadhus. They beg, sing, and are fortune tellers as well. They read palms or sell medicinal herbs or potions.

Some, not real Sadhus, might approach you and if you want a photo with them, you can pay for it. Some members of the group had a photo with one or more of these Sadhus, I did not. I recalled this practice in Rome when I was 25, visiting the Holy City, so long ago.

If you have time you can see the cremation ceremony from beginning to end. The family bring their deceased who are washed and purified in the river as it is considered to be holy water, and then the deceased are ready for the cremation, wrapped in a white cloth and placed above a stone. If the deceased is a woman and her husband is still alive, a red cloth is used. One thing was troubling me and I asked: how do they make sure the person is dead? I was told that they put some water in the deceased's mouth. The family, by respect for the deceased, do not cry and wear white for thirteen weeks.

Monkeys and dogs were wandering everywhere. After leaving Pashupati, we were driven to Boudhanath Stupa, in the centre of Kathmandu.

What is Boudhanath Stupa? It is a huge monument. There are many legends about its origin, though it is believed that it was built during the 5th Century A.D. This Stupa is one of the many UNESCO World Heritages listed monuments in Nepal and the most venerated and holiest Tibetan Buddhist Temple outside Tibet. For the Buddhist pilgrims, this Stupa symbolizes Budda's path for enlightenment. The Buddha was born in Nepal at Lumbini, in 623 B.C. from King Suddhodhana and Queen Maya Devi. The prince, who became the Buddha, had the name of Prince Siddhartha Gualanri and lived most of his life in Kathmandu. Some of Buddha's remains are buried there.

The base represents the earth, the dome the water and the tower, shaped like a square, fire. There are 13 levels of pinnacles which represent the different stages a human being has to go through before achieving the highest state of extinction of desire and individual consciousness in Buddhist or Hindu religions. Walking around it you might feel a special energy and see many chanting monks with their prayer wheels. The Stupa is surrounded by shops, cafes, alleys, streets, monasteries, colourful buildings and many street vendors' stalls.

After the traditional photo at the base of the Stupa, we returned to our hotel.

On day three, we were taken by tourist bus to Pokhara which is about 200 kilometres from Kathmandu. We said good bye to Helen as she was going to fly to Pokhara. We had the option of travelling to Pokhara by bus or plane. With the exception of Helen, we took the bus and travelled with the locals. It was going to be a long drive of about six or eight hours. Having no knowledge of the Nepalese language, I communicated with a smile. The bus was decorated with deities and painted outside and inside with colourful designs. The roads, two way streets, were very narrow with a lot of twists and turns. They were full of potholes after the earthquake, as they had not been repaired. We travelled bumper to bumper, along the hilly roads and I saw three overturned cars in the yards of some houses. At times, the wheels of the tourist bus seemed to touch the edge of the roads; I could see the valley below with its river, 200 metre drop cliff with a vertical or nearly vertical face and very few guard rails.

The traffic was horrendous and there was barely any space between the vehicles coming from the opposite direction, with only a few centimetres separating the two vehicles. At first, I held my breath, until I saw how skilled the bus driver was and started to relax, though not everyone did, with the exception of the locals who were either sleeping or just relaxing not fazed at all. I decided to enjoy the scenic and breathtaking views, the terraced fields and green forest, and the contours of these incredibly beautiful mountains.

Once you are out of the city, there is a big contrast with the villages, and it looks like poverty is rampant with houses along the roads looking more like shacks. I saw, in the front yard of their lodging, women washing their dishes and children playing among the rocks, dust, dirt, garbage and debris, with no fence to protect them if they decided to wander. A little one was crawling in the dirt towards the road while his Mum was still washing her dishes. I held my breath; I wanted to scream, when the Mum got up and slowly went to pick up her baby: all was well. It must be a recurrent event. Some men were smoking under a pergola; others squatted among piles of slates. Their eyes seemed to be wandering to a faraway place.

The hens and their chicks were roaming freely in the yard, never coming too close to the road, as if their instinct knew what to do and what not to do.

A lot of convenience stores and cafes are along the highway. We stopped at a market and bought some fruit and later on we stopped at a coffee place. It was good to be able to stretch our legs and use the amenities.

As we travelled along the road, still very slowly, I was so surprised to see huge posters all in English and promoting our sweet, fizzy drinks and alcohol. What are we introducing to another culture? Big corporations and their power were changing the world. Naively I did not expect this in a Buddhist country and I was flabbergasted.

We crossed a bridge and saw smiling women in their traditional clothing waving a fish in their hands, hoping for someone to stop and buy it. Some local women in bare feet were carrying huge baskets on their backs full of grass or hay or heavy goods while some young students came out from a shop, in school uniforms, showing me that the life for women has changed in this remote part of the world. Indeed, Nepal was predominantly patriarchal, women were subordinate to men. A huge change has occurred since young girls have been allowed to go to school. Nowadays, women are taking leading roles and participating in decision making at all levels. It was so nice to see these young girls living so far away from the city but be able to go to school as I had been told that the change in the countryside was taking a long time, and nothing much had been achieved yet.

Eight hours later, after a bumpy ride, we arrived at Pokhara, with an altitude of 915 metres. There were quite a few Nepalese people in the square. As we got out of the bus, they started to shout and chanted to our surprise: "The Dalai Lama". We did not know if we should laugh or what, so I decided to join my hands and bow respectfully to them. What a welcome! Thank you Pokhara!

After being driven to our hotel, we met our guide, and our four young porters. They would be our walking companions for the next few days. We took possession of our individual room. Nothing was planned for the rest of the day so Helen, Diana, June, Juliet and I decided to visit Pokhara, a modern tourist place, with many shops, cafes and restaurants, in huge contrast to the countryside. It is called the City of Paradise and

Capital of Gandaki Pradesh. Pokhara, a freshwater lake is in the middle of town, surrounded by three of the ten highest mountains of the world in the Himalayas. It is not as busy as Kathmandu; though full of tourists from around the world who wish to trek in the region. It is the gateway to the world for famous hiking and trekking routes.

The following morning, I woke up early; it was still dark. A little bit of day light was piercing the dark night sky. I witnessed the awakening of a new day at Pokhara, as the rays of the rising sun started to shine on Machhapuchhare peak, commonly known as the Fish Tail, and the Annapurna Mountain ranges. It was such a magical moment. As I was looking around, I saw a dome behind a mountain; it was the dome of the Peace Temple. It is a sacred site, on the top of Ananda Hill. What beautiful scenery! My mind wondered: what will I be able to see next?

As the day dawned, the sunshine lit the city below. To my amazement, there was no one on the street, no cars, no trucks, no lorries, no movement, nothing, like if the city was still asleep, or just taking its time to wake up, no busyness. It was such a difference with Australia, where at the crack of dawn, we have to hurry to arrive at work, dropping the children, beforehand, at day-care before school. It was so peaceful and calm. With all my heart, I embraced the stillness of the city and its peacefulness.

After breakfast, we were driven to Nayapul which is at an altitude of 1,050 metres, 45 km from Pokhara. Nayapul is a small village. The main street is a dirt road with coloured shops, tea-rooms, hotels and houses, on each side of the road. All of us were eager to start our first walk which would take us to Tikhedhunga at 1,577 metres, via Birethanti. We would carry a day pack while our young porters, who looked so very young, would carry our backpacks. I heard that the youngest was 17 years old. At one end of the village, there was a beautiful waterfall that looked like the colour of a glacier. The water flowed through boulders, so beautiful to the eyes. We arrived in front of a suspended metal bridge, over the Modi River.

If you are frightened of heights, hold your breath. The suspension bridge is made of two main cables anchored at each end of the bridge. To cross it you walk on metal plates with some spaces between each plate, there is not much protection on each side as the bridge is supported with small cables on each side under the walking plates. I have to tell you, the suspension bridge was long. There was so much vegetation on the other side; I could not see the end of it. Its width was about one metre. I was wondering what would happen when I reached the middle of the bridge if the wind started blowing furiously. How would I stand up? Would the bridge swing? It was an eerie feeling. I had seen this type of bridge in documentaries on television, and now I was going to walk across one of them. Courage Claude, breathe in, breathe out. Slowly, slowly I made it to the other side, while some locals coming in the opposite direction walked on it with such ease. As we met, they smiled at me, and their smile gave me courage. I smiled back and kept on walking with a more positive attitude. A new experience achieved. Being on terra firma was a good feeling. A bit further in the trek we had to cross a small stream over slippery boulders.

We kept on ascending and descending the mountain, past terraced fields. We crossed many villages with their colourful stone houses, with tin roofs held down by stones. What a clever idea, indeed. The roofs can be held down on windy days. Women were working in front of their house straining some grains with huge sieves. Nothing would have changed here over the centuries, all was done manually.

While descending a little section, not a steep one mind you, I fell. Oh dear, I looked around, relieved that none of the group had seen me. I got up as fast as I could. Well at 71, you do not get up so fast in comparison with a 20 year old. I started walking again. I bet I will have a bruise as a souvenir, nothing much really. At a steep hill on a dirt road, a very old, little truck passed me. It was the first vehicle I had seen that day and the last one for the next few days. I was so surprised that they could drive on such road, and going up was one thing, what about going down?

At one stage we climbed some steps built with irregular stones. I looked at our young porters, with their shoes unfit for trekking, and felt sorry for them to have to climb these steps with two heavy backpacks; however they did not seem to have any problem at all and kept on smiling and climbing with ease.

The trek was getting busier, with porters, guides and trekkers. I saw my first donkeys carrying bottles of water and food. Dear me, they overtook me. Surprised! No. The donkeys will do the carting, transporting all the goods necessary for the needs of the inhabitants of the little villages, tea-houses, lodges and conveying many cartons of water bottles for the trekkers. We reached another suspended bridge. This time the metal plates were smaller and closer to each other. The protection on each side resembled strong chicken wire held by metal posts. With more confidence I crossed it, though under my feet, maybe 100 metres or more, there was a river, icy blue in colour surrounded by huge boulders. At the end of the suspended bridge, there was a lovely traditional Nepalese village with a beautiful waterfall Tikhedhunga, at an altitude of 1,577 metres. We stayed in a mountain lodge, a real palace, in comparison with local houses. After a shower, we met in the dining room area for our evening meal. Around the room you could hear so many different languages, and I loved it. I was surprised to see that they provided not only for vegetarians but for non-vegetarians, being a Buddhist and Hindu country. To my amazement, our young porters did not join us, though they could speak some English and I would have liked very much to learn more about their culture. If you had a mobile phone, you were able to recharge it.

The next morning after breakfast, we started our third trekking day. We would finish it at Ghorepani. We crossed another suspension bridge and started to climb. Remember I had to climb 365 steps to reach the Monkey Temple in Kathmandu. Well, it is better not to know what is ahead of you, just like in life. Most of this climb was made of stone steps lining the side of the mountain. Was I puffing? Puffing would not be the word, I would have used! It was so hard. The stone steps were uneven and never ending. Soon I could see a quaint little village with its inhabitants calmly going about their daily chores: I thought this had to be the last step. No way, there were still more and more in front of me. I was not the only one to huff and puff I can assure you. It was a real 'killer'.

I wanted to take more photos, but with my track record from my previous trek in Australia, I did not take too many. Thankfully, we had incredible, unimaginable, unforgettable views and landscapes which helped me, for a few seconds only put out of my mind the difficulty of the ascent. The donkeys were passing me with their huge loads with such ease that I wished to be one of them, but just for a little while, and obviously returning as a human at the end of the day!

After a sharp ascent we arrived at Ulleri, an ancient settlement, at an altitude of 1,960 metres, with terraced farm lands. We had to traverse another suspended bridge. By then it felt as if I was a local, as I had lost my fear, therefore it was not a problem anymore. We saw more waterfalls and kept on climbing more and more steps up to Banthanti, at an altitude of 2,210 metres where we stopped for lunch. As we went through the village, a young lady was squatting in front of a tap of water, and doing her dishes on the side of the street while another one was washing her clothes and sheets by hand. It was probably the only water point for the village. I could just imagine how cold the water would have been.

They kept on doing their chores smiling and their faces looking completely at peace. What a contrast with us, who have a washing machine to do this tedious task. I have to tell you that in our modern world, the electric appliance that is most important to me is the washing machine.

I could manage not having any other modern conveniences, but the washing machine. I am so grateful to James King who invented a drum device, in 1851, for the first washing machine. I have to say he carried well his name, as for me he is a 'King' and Alva J. Fisher, who invented the first powered washing machine in 1908.

Back to the walk. We started going down on stone steps, and rocky paths, and crossed thick, dense, beautiful forests of oak trees and rhododendrons. Crossing this forest in spring with the incredible colours of the rhododendron flowers would have been out of this world. The rhododendron is the national flower of Kathmandu. Many birds were serenading us with their enchanting songs.

Was I tired or what? I started to walk slower. My asthma was giving me trouble, and I found myself away from the group. I was not frightened as there was only one path, and it was impossible to get lost. When I reached the top of a small hill, I saw the group down below. I decided to cross the mountain downhill diagonally, not along the path, and this way I would be able to catch up with the group. There were a lot of wet leaves and some fallen trees. All went well, until one member, seeing me crossing the hill this way, shouted: 'Claude'. I jumped, lost my balance and rolled down the hill. Landing at the bottom of the hill, seeing the members' worried faces, I got up as fast as I could, smiling to everyone, saying I was ok. In fact I was not. I had a pain in my chest and had breathing difficulties. I had seen worse, and thought that in a little while I would feel better and kept on walking. Juliet noticed that I was in a bit of trouble and decided to walk with me. I did not want to show her how painful my chest was so I started joking with Juliet. A bit later, I lost my balance again, and we laughed and laughed, hiding my discomfort.

As we crossed the forest we still had more stone steps and rocky path to climb up. I could not believe it. The climb became not as steep but winding just the same and gradually, we reached our destination, Ghorepani, at an altitude of 2,870 metres. Though not that big, it is the largest village of the Annapurna with an excellent view of the Himalayas. It had been a very challenging, dare I say 'killer' day and I told Juliet: "From now on, I do not want to see or climb steps anymore". Though the trail was absolutely beautiful with its picturesque mountains, villages, waterfalls, and clear streams, it was not an easy walk. I learnt we had climbed up to 3,700 steps that day, mostly uphill. Yes, 3,700 steps.

I congratulated myself, 'good on you girl' and, at the same time, trying to ignore the thought that we will have to climb down them again.

I shared a room with Juliet that night. I did not sleep very well at all, as lying flat on the Nepalese bed made my breathing so much more painful. I did not dare move in case I woke her up. The next morning, I saw many bruises on my legs, my chest, and I started to feel pins and needles in my hands, but still keeping quiet about my predicament. From then on, Juliet stayed and walked with me till the end of our journey. We joked and laughed a lot, even though my chest was very painful.

The next morning, an icy morning, and it was still pitch black, we left Ghorepani. The main street was so alive, everyone was up. The torches or headlights looked like little moving stars as the trekkers meandered through the village. This section would take us to Poon Hill, at an altitude of 3,210 metres: the highlight of the trek. That section was supposed to be easier. It was not the case for me - more steps to climb, and the altitude was affecting me more. I started to feel pins and needles in my head; the ones in my hands got worse, plus my breathing was getting shallower. That section of the trek was bustling with trekkers, with their guides or porters. Gradually, I made it to the top on time to see the sunrise. On the platform, there were hundreds of trekkers of many nationalities waiting for the sunrise.

Like everyone, I was holding my breath, as the magic of nature started to arise, behind the mountain ranges. The first rays of the sun appeared with yellow, more golden and red colours. Gradually, as the sun rose, more magical moments happened in front of my eyes, as I discovered such mesmerizing views of the highest mountain in the world with its snow-capped peaks.

I was speechless. It was a breathtaking and magical scene, 360 degrees of the highest mountains with a crisp blue sky for backdrop. In front of me were the most beautiful mountain peaks, the Annapurna at 8,091 metres, the Dhaulagiri Himalayas 8,167 metres. The Dhaulagiri is the 7th highest mountain in the world and lies entirely within Nepal. Then appeared the Machhapuchhare Mountain (Fish Tail), at 6,993 metres, the first mountain I saw in Pokhara. These gigantic mountains were in front of me, I was spellbound.

No matter what, I had made it. All the exhaustion, the pain, the puffing, the falls, all had been worth it and rewarding. I was gob-smacked, mesmerised by such a beauty of nature and an incredible feeling of peace and calmness entered my soul. One could think it was due to the exhaustion but it was much more: a deeper, more powerful feeling of happiness and blissfulness. I let this amazing sensation enter my whole mind and body and embraced it with open arms, the power of nature, thanking God or the Universe for giving us such beauty for us to admire. It was another fascinating moment in my life.

From the top of the world, I thanked my daughter, as without her phone call I would not have lived such an incredible moment.

It was time to return and hike back down to Ghorepani for breakfast. We had more steps to climb, up and downhill. Still on cloud nine, I enjoyed the spectacular views and took it all in. Back at the lodge we all chatted around the table, amazed by this miraculous event we had just witnessed. We recharged our mobiles and collected our bags before starting the walk to Tadapani, at an altitude of 2,675 metres.

As we left Ghorepani, to my disbelief, there were more and more steep stairs to walk up along the edge of the lush green mountain while still seeing the Annapurna ranges with its snow-capped peak. I had the impression that they were getting closer, even if I knew if it was an optical illusion: I was in awe.

More beautiful and outstanding landscapes and valleys between mountains reminded me of my country of birth. My chest was hurting and so painful, but I had no time to rest as there were still more steep steps to climb even in the middle of dense forests. The fog started to close in when we descended to the valley and a few kilometres later, it lifted. As we know, mountains are mountains and they are unpredictable. Everywhere, Buddhist prayer flags were suspended from one tree to the next, or across the path. Eventually, we came to a platform with blissful panoramic views. I decided to take a breather there. The pins and needles in my hands and head were getting worse, and just the fact of holding my trekking poles was getting more difficult. I was hoping that with a bit of rest, they would lessen. It was wishful thinking. I tried to put the pain out of my mind as I did not want to lose the beautiful experience I had at the top of the world and slowly I started walking again along the stairs and rocky paths. I arrived last but I did not mind at all. I never shared with anyone my experience. The determination, some will call stubbornness that I discovered while crossing France and Spain, on foot, seven years earlier and what I had experienced walking the Larapinta Trail had kicked in. No way would I share what was happening in my body. I kept climbing up and down stairs, stone paved trails and rocky paths, passing in front of beautiful shrines. I was still so cold even being on the trail all the time. Crossing small wooden bridges we passed through small, charming villages. It felt like the locals were looking at life passing by, smiling, relaxed they looked so happy without any worry in the world, some would say: 'Namaste', which was so lovely and warming.

Finally we arrived at the small village of Tadapani, with its roofs of blue tin, nestled below the Sacred and famous Machhapuchhare Mountain, the Fish Tail. It is considered to be the place of God where Lord Shiva resides. It has never been climbed to the top by any human. It is so respected that even the first British team who attempted the climb in 1957 never completed it, as they had made a promise to the king of the time to not set foot on the actual summit. It was an unforgettable and mystical sight. I decided to approach our guide, Anch, and inform him about the pins and needles in my hands and head. He replied:

'Claude you have altitude sickness'.

I looked at him, surprised and doubted how I could have altitude sickness since I had not vomited.

'Claude, have you got any Diamox or tablets for altitude sickness'.

'Yes' was my answer.

I was flabbergasted: 'Altitude Sickness?' I kept to myself about the pain in my chest. Sleeping flat was becoming unbearable. I was too scared to say anything about it, in case Anch would call a helicopter and send me to the hospital.

We all met, tired and very happy in the communal dining room, overwhelmed by what we had witnessed. We had been blessed with a crisp, cold day without any rain and unforgettable sights and sunrise. We were overpowered by the beauty of this region. It was Anch's birthday and we took the opportunity to celebrate his birthday. What a way to finish this incredible, majestic day.

The next morning we left for Ghandruk, at an altitude of 2,010 metres, with a clear sky. We were climbing down more stairs, and more stairs. The pins and needles had not left me. I would have to endure them no matter what and psych myself up, as my chest was still hurting so much while trekking. Juliet stayed with me; we went through more rhododendrons, oaks and dense forests. In some small areas covered with grass we saw some huge buffalos called 'Yaks' grazing. We passed them, and they did not even look at us. At one stage, our guide, Anch, told us to be very quiet, and not to talk and he showed us two grey monkeys, called langurs, sitting on the branches of a tree. If you make too much noise, they jump as quickly as a flash to other branches, maybe they are shy, or maybe they don't like to be disturbed by humans!

I was so enchanted by the sounds of the birds, the waterfalls, the gorges. We crossed more streams over rocks and small wooden bridges, more paved stones, and descents and steep ascents, still following the breathtaking views of the Annapurna mountain ranges. It felt like they were our walking companions and had an eye on us or wanted to protect us.

After three or four hour's walk we arrived at Ghandruk village, still in the shadow of the Annapurna mountain ranges and the Machhapuchhare Mountain. The last few days we crossed very quiet, tranquil villages with hens and roosters wandering in the middle of the main street made only of stairs, no highways or roads, the stairs being the only road. The adults, like the children, were so agile and fast walking down or up the stairs, it seemed like it was nothing for them. I wished I could have been able to climb the stairs with the same agility. The inhabitants were doing their daily work without the pressure of the outside world or the city, just letting life pass by, quietly, living at their own pace: no rush was necessary. They looked so calm, and peaceful, though life would not have been so easy in this high altitude the whole year around and especially during the winter months. Humans are amazing, adapting to cold, heat, humidity and so on.

Ghandruk was so unlike the other villages we had crossed the previous days, it was bustling; it is the second largest village in Nepal. The roofs were not made of tin anymore but covered with slate and the houses were built of bricks or stones. It is the home of the ethnic group called 'Gurung'. They have kept their own traditions and cultures. In front of their houses, were paved terraces; the women, in a squatting position, were beating the rice and milled stalks with a stick and letting the grains fall onto a blanket. All was done manually.

We visited the Gurung Museum displaying artefacts, antiques, utensils and woven baskets, and we were able to see and learn firsthand about their culture and way of life.

The 'Gurung' migrated from Mongolia during the 6th century, and are known under the name of 'Tamu". They have their own dialect. Their religion is a mixture of Hinduism, Shamanism and Buddhism. They are farmers and agriculturists growing wheat, rice, millet and potatoes. From the outside, we could see on the second floor of the Museum, a big placard of the copy of a Rs. 1000 bill showing the Museum.

As we were visiting the village, we saw some young boys carrying some hay or other things. Juliet, who had brought some small toys, opened her backpack and gave them some tennis balls.

Right away they started to play with them. Juliet, June and Diana joined in the game with the children, and I observed their joy from the sideline. Their excitement brightened their little faces; it was so warming to see how a simple tennis ball could bring them such happiness.

In the street there was a sign which attracted my attention:

> 'TO ACCOMPLISH GREAT THINGS
> 'YOU MUST NOT ONLY ACT
> 'BUT ALSO DREAM
> 'NOT ONLY PLAN
> 'BUT ALSO BELIEVE.

(Thank you to be part of our recovery G.W.F.)

Back at our Mountain Lodge, as I was going to take my shower that was situated at the end of the walkway, I saw, down below, one of our young porters showing his damaged thongs to one of the other porters. With their gestures, I understood and went straight back to my bedroom, took out my sandals from my backpack, and quickly ran down the stairs. You must know by now what I mean by 'quickly' I asked him to try on my sandals. They fitted him perfectly and I told him to keep them. He refused, but I insisted and before he had the time to give them back to me I had left.

The next day, we left Ghandruk to reach Nayapul, the village from where we had started our unforgettable trek. It was going to be the longest and easiest section of the whole trek. We saw other awesome views of terraced rice fields. The donkeys were still climbing the stairs and transporting all the necessities to the villages, as they were the only means of transport. We descended the path with a gentle decline, slowly, and crossed more friendly villages and streams with their icy blue colour. While we were crossing a village some young children approached us and asked for toys. We were in a very isolated area, and not specifically rich, but to our surprise most of the inhabitants had mobile phones. It was not Chinese whispers but near enough. They had received a message on their phone saying: 'that someone in our group had toys and had given some to the children of the village'. To their delight, Juliet was able to give them some. We were so happy to see their smiling faces and joy.

At one stage we had to go across a small creek over a beam, its width being no more than 25 to 30 cm. Oh My God, another challenge! I must have been still asleep when I heard that it was going to be an easy trek or I must have been dreaming! My heart started to beat fast, very fast, recalling how hopeless I was during my schooling at gymnastics. It was not a long way to cross, maybe eight metres or ten metres. I looked around to see if there was a way out. Unfortunately, no, I had to do it and decided not to look down. Closer to the edge, I saw a little plank had been nailed onto the beam: well that will be a great help. I concentrated, and gradually, slowly, not looking down but ahead, I arrived on the other side, relieved to have made it in one piece. Another challenge won! Then more steps up and down, my body was very, very tired, that is the least I can say. Did I say, a few days before that, I did not want to see any more steps? Hmm!

We were crossing a small village, when for whatever reason; I went into a little shop. On the right hand side of the shop, I saw, to my surprise, a big banner with writing in English: "Happy birthday Anch" and underneath it, around a table, many young school children and their mothers eating a birthday cake. I rushed outside and called Juliet asking her if she still had any toys left for the little boy. She had one. You should have seen this little boy's face when he received his Australian toy and when we sang 'Happy Birthday'. It was magical! I was so grateful to Juliet, who had brought so much joy to all the children we met along the way.

Eventually, we arrived at a small village called 'Syauli Bazaar'. We stopped for a break and enjoyed the magnificent waterfall on the side of the tea-house. The Annapurna Mountain Ranges looked further away. More terraced fields, the farmers reassembled the dried stalks of wheat, rice and millet to build domes in the shape of small houses.

From 'Syauli Bazaar' Anch, our guide told us that the trek was going to be easy from then on: flat all the way. When we arrived at Nayapul, I approached Anch and told him, my understanding of the meaning of flat was not the same as his, and once I was back to Australia I would have to check in the Oxford Dictionary the meaning of 'flat'. We had a good laugh. We had walked the entire loop and now we were driven back to Pokhara but not to the same hotel.

The next morning, from our first experience, we knew what time we would leave, but not what time we would arrive. We, Westerners, live every second of the day with our eyes on our watch, the Nepalese don't. What is important for them is that they arrive at their destination, not what time they arrive at their destination. It was quite refreshing and so relaxing except if you had to arrive on time at the airport!

The road was jammed with traffic both ways busy: dusty, with potholes, as many sections are not sealed. At times, the dust was so thick that we could not see the road. The trees close to the road had their leaves covered with thick grey dust. There were many teahouses, and small shops all along the road; the little shacks were the lodgings of many families with the hens and their little ones scratching for food in the dirt in the front courtyards, along with wandering dogs, geese and ducks. It took us four hours to arrive at Pokhara which is only 45 kilometres from Nayapul.

In the dining room of the hotel we spent some time with our young porters and our guide Anch. At the exception of Anch, our guide, we would not be seeing the others anymore, as they were returning to their village and families. An envelope passed between the group and each of us put some money in, to be shared equally among the porters.

They were wonderful young men, carrying our backpacks, always smiling and polite, and not being bothered by the number of kilos they were carrying on their backs. They were so conscientious. The only thing I regret, is not sharing our evening meals with them. It was a missed opportunity to know more about their culture. We said good-bye wishing them a lovely future.

The next day, after breakfast we were driven to Chitwan National Park. The conditions of the road were still the same and sadly I saw more pollution: plastic water bottles, garbage bags, and paper. I decided not to look at the road anymore but to enjoy the scenery, with the mountains covered with green forests, and the river down below. I was embracing everything when suddenly we came to a standstill. We all looked at each other wondering what was happening; the bus driver was still very calm, smiling: no worries.

We waited for a long while, staying still, puzzled and wondering, when a bulldozer tried to make its way between the cars and trucks in both directions. Our bus driver could not move as we were too close to the edge, but the upcoming vehicles did. I was so amazed that they managed to get closer to the side of the mountain, as it seemed there was no space left at all, but somehow they did. Eventually we started to move again. We arrived near a village, when to my surprise, I saw the bulldozer had pushed a truck on the side of the road, as it had broken down, and stopped all traffic. The bulldozer had replaced what we call 'roadside assistance'!

I smiled, loving it, it was so ingenious. Our driver was never stressed, or appeared not to be stressed, and kept on smiling. As we travelled, we saw people paragliding and canoeing along the river below. Finally after six hours on the road, we reached Chitwan National Park which is 150 km from Pokhara.

We were welcomed at our lodging, in a beautiful setting, by the owner and his smiling courteous staff. Inside the property there was a magnificent garden with so many varieties of plants some were in bloom, a real delight to the eyes. I received my room keys. To my surprise, I had a room by myself, and on the key ring the word 'Bliss' was written, I smiled as the word "Bliss" was part of the title of my first book.

A little while later we went walking to the river. We had to cross the main road, and saw the doors of a shop completely damaged, as if a truck had gone through it. We were told that an elephant would have done this damage during the night and not to go and wander in the town after 20:00 or 8.00pm as the elephants usually roamed in the town looking for food.

The next morning we visited an elephant sanctuary. It was sad to see the elephant chained, but I understood why, after seeing what had happened to the shop the previous night. I was told by the local police that all the elephants from the reserve were let loose and grazed morning and afternoon. During the day, they stayed in the shade, away from the heat and were chained for safety reasons as many visitors spend time in the National Park. It was, indeed, very busy.

As we were walking in the sanctuary, a group of young men, students I presumed, asked me to have a photo taken with them. I obliged gracefully, to their delight. It was like a repeat of what had happened at the Monkey Temple and I thought: 'My grey hair creates magic'!

We left the sanctuary and walked along the river when, to our amazement, we saw an enormous one horned Rhinoceros, with what looked like a plated armour on its back. The one-horned rhinoceros is protected; it was near extinction some years ago, but nowadays no more, thanks to a good program of preservation. Scrutinising the water we saw another one grazing along the river bank. It was an amazing sight.

We had to go across the river, and to do so we needed to go over a bridge again. This one was pretty precarious. The platform was made of bamboo sticks covered with sandbags. On each side you had strong sticks, but not too big, attached to the bamboo from the platform with leather bands, then two rows of small tree-trunks, attached to each other. You would hold your breath, I assure you. Looking back, the first bridges I had come across seemed so incredibly safe. I had become such a brave girl! And I walked across without any problem.

The Chitwan's indigenous people are called Tharu, and live as a community. They have their own culture, tradition, and way of life, their own beliefs, and language which are related to nature. After our evening meal we were invited to go to the Tharu Cultural Centre and assisted at a presentation of their cultural dances, in their diverse traditional costumes. As they performed, they used long and short sticks. The funniest dance was the peacock dance. When it was over, we returned to our lodging. Crossing the main street, a young girl in a shop sitting on a blanket on the floor, was doing her homework and probably looking after the shop too.

The next morning, after breakfast, we set out again for a full day in Chitwan National Park, which is a protected area and World Heritage listed site since 1979. It is a rich natural area with dense forest, marshlands and grassland along the river banks. A few of our group enjoyed an elephant-riding safari. These elephants are kept in the hotel ground. In an enclosure, the rest of the group and I decided to opt for a walk in the jungle. It was fabulous; there were so many butterflies and birds with amazing colours, an absolute paradise for bird lovers.

We, then, went canoeing along the river banks. There were only few huts. Only very few locals are allowed to live on the banks of the river. A young woman in traditional dress was washing her clothes by hand in the river. No one was talking, absorbing the peacefulness, hearing only the regular rhythm and sound of the paddle touching the water. We reached the other side of the river where our jeep tour in the jungle was to start. Once in the jeep we crossed the rich, dense and sub-tropical jungle. We were fortunate to see a lot of deer, wild pigs, hanuman langurs (monkeys), squirrels, crocodiles, bears, birds, butterflies and many mammals.

After this incredible morning, we enjoyed watching the elephants bathing; I fed one with the green bananas I bought from a seller on the bank of the river. I patted the elephant, and was surprised to find out how coarse its skin was. I decided to have a chat with it, and had the feeling it could understand me, as its eyes looked deeply into mine. What an experience! Helen and Juliet decided to get on top of an elephant. This cheeky one pumped some water from the river with its trunk and showered them. Helen and Juliet were shocked and stunned, while the crowd on the edge of the beach laughed heartily.

The next morning we were driven back by private bus to our hotel in Kathmandu, a ten hour drive. Some kilometres into the drive, our driver asked us if we would like to see a very long bridge and we walked along it. As we had all become such experts at this, we decided to do it. We walked through the courtyard of some houses and stairs.

It was a bit like a maze. I am sure no one, with the exception of the locals, would have found this path. Was it a long bridge? Maybe 200 or 300 metres long at least, and the same type of swaying bridge I had mentioned before. As confident as a local, I walked back and forth. I loved it. I had conquered a few more of my fears during that trek!

Along the road, I was very sad to see so much pollution. In one area, monkeys were scavenging among the mountains of rubbish. At that moment, there was a big bend and I read on the side of the truck in front of us: 'Pray for Nepal'

When we arrived at the hotel the tour company manager, Arjun, was there and invited all of us for dinner at a restaurant. Some dancers performed traditional dances with their traditional musical instrument. The backdrop of the stage represented the Annapurna with the Fish Tail Mountain. Their dances were somewhat different from the ones we saw at Chitwan as were their costumes. I would say they were gentler, heart-warming dances. I enjoyed their performance very much. At the end of the show, they asked if any guests would like to come to the stage and dance with the traditional dancers. I stayed put while some members went onto the stage.

During the meal, some members of another group joined us. It is at this point that Diana informed me that she had booked a flight over Mount Everest for the following morning. I told her I would love to do it, but I did not have enough cash on me to cover the cost. I had tried to take some money out from a few ATM's without any success as my card did not allow me to withdraw any money. Diana kindly offered to pay for my ticket if there was an available seat on the plane. The manager of the tour company, Arjun, was present, and I approached him. No problem, he said, I will deal with this. He came back a little while later and informed me that he had booked a seat. I was ecstatic; tomorrow I would be flying over Mount Everest. I was very grateful to Diana and on my return to Brisbane I transferred the money to her bank account.

The next day, we said goodbye to Helen, Nola and Paul as they were flying back to Australia and New Zealand, while Diana and I were driven to the airport. The airline company was Buddha Air, a perfect name for Nepal, I thought. I was thrilled and somewhat impatient to see Mount Everest from an aeroplane.

On the plane, each person had a window seat, a real treat this allowed everyone to have an unobstructed view. As we flew over Kathmandu I could see the sprawling city, unfortunately with a cloud of dust over it.

In the plane we were able to go left and right to take photos, as well as visit the cockpit and have a chat with the pilots, if we wanted to. That was incredible. In no time, we were close to the Himalayas. I was seeing glaciers, twenty of the highest peaks in the world and Mount Everest in all its beauty. Though we did not circle the Himalayas or go over Mount Everest, I was dumbstruck by such a breathtaking view. It had been a one hour scenic and magical flight.

Back at the hotel, I decided to go and walk in Kathmandu, while Diana and June went to do some errands, as they were flying back home the following morning. While wandering in the city for some presents I met two young French people: Alexandre and Florence. They were cycling around the world. Oh, dear! What courage and endurance! They had done the eighteen day trek in Annapurna and had found it hard.

On my way back, in the Thamel centre, not far from the hotel, a young Nepalese girl was selling some little silk bags that she had probably sewn herself and other gadgets. I decided to purchase a few things. As I was going to pay, I realised that I did not have enough change on me. I had left some money in my hotel room, and I told her to put aside my purchases. I insisted to trust me and said:

'I promise you, I will be back'.

On the way to my room, I thought that maybe this young Nepalese girl used the sales of the day to care for and feed her whole family or maybe she was living from day to day, relying on the sales. At that point, I decided to do something for her.

Walking back, I knew from the bottom of my heart I was doing the right thing, I had to help. As she saw me, she smiled at me, and I smiled back. It was possible that she was not sure that I would return. In her hand she was holding a necklace. Getting closer to her, she took my hand, like if she wanted to give me the necklace. I pretended that I did not understand and ignored her gesture. I told her that I would love for her to come with me to the shop close by and buy whatever she wanted for her and her family and asked the security guard who was there to look after her display while we went to do some shopping. Kindly he agreed. Hand in hand we went to the shop and Chanti bought some cakes for her and her family maybe these were a special treat for them, I did not ask.

She was still holding in her hand the necklace and from time to time she tried to take my hand to give me the necklace, looking into my eyes and said: 'Yes, from me to you'. I kept ignoring her gesture and kept smiling at her. Back at her little stand, I gave her the money for my purchases. At that moment, she grabbed my hand, opened it and put the necklace in it. I wanted to give her some money for it, but she refused with force in her voice.

At that time, I remembered an event which happened a few years ago when I refused the gift of a banana from a Muslim female client, at the hospital where I am volunteering. As I left the room, a male member of the family informed my refusal was considered as an insult. I had thought they were depriving themselves of food for me. Two cultures seeing things differently, I had thought to be kind in refusing. My heart was hurting.

Back to my story with Chanti, I held the necklace; I put it on my heart then Chanti put it around my neck. I was so touched, tears flowed down my cheeks. Chanti had shown me so much love, probably she had nothing and was struggling to feed her family, but she had a heart of gold. What a lesson for all of us!

I hugged her and left. The security guard seeing this approached us and said to Chanti: 'this woman is special and is a very kind lady'. In reality, who was kind and loving: Chanti or me? I can tell you, for me it was Chanti. I walked back to the hotel feeling so humble. I treasure Chanti's necklace.

Back at the hotel, I ran into Juliet, who was worried about a purchase she had made and realised it may not be ready prior to her departure the following morning. I suggested she show me the shop as I could go and collect it for her and I would mail it to her once I was back in Australia. When we arrived at the jeweller's shop, her present was ready. While Juliet was talking with the jeweller, I looked around and saw a medal, similar to the one I had seen in O'Ceibrero – Spain, I could not believe it. At the time I wanted it so much, but did not buy it as I thought I would find it again somewhere along the way or in Santiago. And here it was, in front of me, not in Spain but, in Nepal. I was flabbergasted. I could not take my eyes off this piece. The salesman noticed it:

'Do you want to buy this medal?'

Still gobsmacked, I replied with a nod of my head: 'Yes'. Once he told me the price, I had to decline, as I did not have enough money on me, once more. How much have you got? I emptied my purse in front of him and he said:

'You remind me of my mother – all is well, you can have it'

Then he added:

'When you give, you receive'

I thanked him profusely feeling so blessed. The salesman had said the same words than Mohamed, a Muslim from Morocco living in France, when he gave me some mandarins while I was walking the Saint James' Way.

From my hotel, I rang Prakashik. We would meet the next morning at 8.00am. In the evening, I went to a restaurant close to the hotel with Julie. There, on the terrace, I saw garlands of shells hanging around the flower pots. For the second time that day, events brought me back to my pilgrimage when, at the age of 64, I crossed France and Spain, alone, along the Saint James' Way, for 100 days. How strange to see these garlands made with shells which are the symbols of the Saint-James' Way, here. Were they messages? More to ponder!

Prakashik arrived on time for our trip, and to my surprise, not wearing his monk's robe but dressed like a westerner. We were going to visit the temple I had seen at the top of a mountain the first day I had arrived in Kathmandu. To my surprise, Prakashik had ordered a taxi. We drove for about 20 minutes from the Thamel Center, to reach the entrance of the Shivapuri Nagarjun National Park, where we had to pass a check point. In Nepal, the drivers have to be so skilful on these narrow, dirt roads full of potholes. I asked if we could hike to the top of the Nagarjun Hill. We could. Prakashik did not think it was wise as there were Indian Leopards and wild bears in the Park, and we could meet them. He did not want anything happening to me. It was so sweet and considerate of him. There was such kindness in his eyes. I was very touched.

The Nagarjun Hill is a subtropical, dense forest full of oaks and rhododendron trees. The colourful birds were everywhere in the sprawling forest as well as Langurs (monkeys), snakes (cobras) and as mentioned above, leopards and wild bears. It is the last woodland left in the Kathmandu Valley.

There were quite a few visitors at the top of the mountain. Prayer flags were floating in every corner. There was a small Stupa which had been built for Ach Arya Nagarjun Buddha. It is a place of worship for Buddhists and Hindus. Some lighted candles were burning in front of the statue. We visited the temple with its beautiful painting of deities.

Afterwards we climbed up a staircase. From there, we could embrace a breathtaking and magnificent view of the Annapurna and Himalayas. A feeling of peacefulness and calmness embraced us. Walking around the mountain, I abruptly stopped, as my eyes noticed a spot, I could not move anymore. I froze. It is said that we dream every night, well I can tell you, and I do not remember my dreams, with the exception of this one. Many years ago, I had dreamed of two monks at the top of a mountain, with the same type and colour of robes worn by Buddhist monks and Prakashik. In my dream, one monk was standing up while the other one was sitting at his feet, both of them looking at the stunning landscape, praying I suppose. I was shaken. The vision in my dream was so vivid that it had stayed with me always, not quite understanding it and here I was remembering it as clear as if it had happened the previous night. I was in a Buddhist country, wasn't I? I did not share any of it with Prakashik. It was too big for me.

My thoughts were about the circumstances, the synchronicity of how I came to trek in Nepal, the meeting that led me to this place, when on our way down, I heard a male voice shouting: 'Grandma – Grandma'. Stunned, I looked around, knowing that could not be my grandson, Alexander. In fact, it was a young Nepalese man, who was waving at me and I met Ash.

Eventually we left, and drove back to Kathmandu. Prakashik and I went for lunch in a Tibetan restaurant as at the Nararjun temple there was no tea-house or restaurant. We enjoyed each other's company. Prakashik had to return to the monastery by 3.00pm so we went to the Boudhanath Stupa and walked around it. Before returning to the hotel and in front of the Stupa, Prakashik asked me if we could see each other again. I informed him that I would be flying back the next day but we could meet early in the morning.

I was waiting for Prakashik in the lobby of the hotel, when I saw a Nepalese newspaper Kathmandu Post, translated into English. On the page: 'Free the words'

I was reading an article 'Down to Earth' by Menila Kharel words about 'how farming used to be done in a humble way by the Indigenous without chemicals which deteriorate our health'. There is a balance to re-create a healthy soil which will not affect the health of human beings. I smiled as a few days ago, I had shared with the group how farming was done when I was young and probably still nowadays at some farms in France.

Living in the mountains, the cattle were brought back every night to the stable, and before winter they were not allowed out, due to the snow and to give the fields a chance to rest and regenerate. The cattle were fed with hay that the farmers had grown during the summer. Every day, second grade hay was laid over the concrete so the cattle would not feel the cold and every morning, the soiled hay was collected and placed in an area not far from the stable, replaced by a fresh layer of clean hay. Through a channel the urine was collected and directed to an underground concrete tank. As I was sharing these memories of my youth, I saw some of the members frowning. I smiled as I knew how they would react when they heard the rest as they lived in the city. Every spring, the urine collected during the year was sprayed over the field, then the soiled hay that had been maturing for months, was put back to the soil to fertilize it before planting the new crop. What I predicted happened, as I heard 'Yuk, yuk'. I told them that is organic farming. I thought it was a shame that all the members had left, they could have read the article.

I had just finished reading the article in the newspaper when Prakashik arrived. In his hand was a beautiful yellow shawl and he asked me to put it on my altar at home. I felt so blessed and privileged. I thanked him and talked a bit longer before we had to separate, as he had to return to the monastery. I never told him about my dream. I did not have an altar at home but I put it over a painting that my daughter had given me many years ago for Mother's Day. It represents mountains, rivers, lakes, forests and fields, exactly like my journey in Nepal.

I ordered a taxi to drive me to the airport; the traffic was horrendous and I started to get seriously worried, wondering if I would ever arrive on time, though I had left the hotel well early. At last we arrived. I went through customs pretty fast and learnt that the plane had a delay of three hours. I was changing planes in Singapore. I was so stressed. When I landed in

Singapore I had only a short time to get on my next plane, somehow I did it but I do not know how.

On my arrival back to Brisbane, I went to my doctor I had an X-Ray, which revealed a small fissure along a rib and bruising. During the trek, I was somewhat affected by my asthma. The pins and needles eventually disappeared.

The Itinerary: 11 Days Poon Hill

Day	From/To	Distance	Time	Altitude
1	Sightseeing Kathmandu	–	–	1,345m
2	Kathmandu – Pokhara (200 kms) by bus	–	–	915m
3	Pokhara – Nayapul – Tikhedhunga	7km	3hrs trekking	1,050m - 1,577m

Day	From/To	Distance	Time	Altitude
4	Tikhedhunga – Ghorepani	12km	7hrs trekking	2,675m
5	Ghorepani – Poon Hill – Tadapani	10km	6hrs trekking	3,210m - 2,675m
6	Tadapani – Ghandruk	9.5km	3hrs trekking	1,950m
7	Ghandruk – Nayapul (Drive back Nayapul –Pokhara)	18km	4hrs trekking	1,050m
8	Pokhara – Chitwan	150km	Drive	–
9	Chitwan Jungle (Activities)	–	–	–
10	Chitwan Kathmandu	180km	Drive	–
11	Kathmandu – Visit Temple at Nagarjun Hill with Prakashik	–		–

CHAPTER 3

Walking with Camino Skies' group in Spain

The Camino Frances – Saint-Jean-Pied-De-Port – Santiago de Compostela

34 days: 12 April 2018 – 17 May 2018
at 72 years of age

How did it happen? 26 February 2017, I launched the Australian Premiere of the movie 'Looking for infinity: El Camino', from Aaron C. Leaman, at Six Cinemas - New Farm, Brisbane, which led me to direct more Q and A's around Brisbane and some other parts of Australia.

In July 2017, I again launched Aaron's movie at Avoca Beach in New South Wales, Australia, and on my return home after introducing the movie, I received a phone call from Fergus Grady who informed me that he would like very much for me to be part of his project: doing a documentary about the Camino in 2018. Needless to say, I was quite surprised. Fergus and I had been in contact since 2015, before my involvement in my first Q and A for the International Best Seller movie: 'Six Ways to Santiago' when it was launched in Brisbane and then for 'Looking for infinity: El Camino', as I asked him if he could help Aaron to promote his movie in Australia. Fergus wanted to launch his career in the film industry. I was hesitant as I had not planned to walk the Camino that year, as well as walking with a group for so many days could be a real challenge. Putting my fear aside after our exchanges I agreed. What played a part in my decision was the fact that I was going to help someone, and walking the Camino again, I did not need much convincing. My first pilgrimage in 2010 had changed my life, as I had discovered the real 'me', leaving my life burdens on the side of the Saint James' Way, and returning anew. Needless to say, the idea of walking the Camino again was very tempting. Whoever has walked the Camino will understand. After walking the Camino, it calls you back and back, I agreed, I would help and be part of it.

As, I had to self-fund my journey and expenses, my only request was to stay in municipal Albergues, local council refuges, to which Fergus agreed.

I flew to Paris in early March. I was taking this opportunity to visit my family in France and Austria. After a few days spent with my sister, Michele, I flew to Vienna, Austria, as my brother, Philippe, lives in Melk and there I met a young Austrian pilgrim, Jonathan. We had met in 2010 along the Camino Frances before Burgos and had stayed in contact. When you meet pilgrims along any Camino, these pilgrims can become part of your Camino family forever. Since 2010, my pilgrims' family has extended, to my great joy.

A few days later, I flew to Geneva, Switzerland. My cousin, Jean-Paul, came to pick me up at the airport, and then we had a Tranchant's family reunion in Annecy (France). Afterwards, I went back to my birth place to pray and visit my Maman (Mum) and Papa's grave and stayed with some school friends, Francine and Suzanne. I had planned to travel by train from my birth town to Saint-Jean-Pied-de-Port. It was not meant to be, with train-strikes in France, and I flew to Biarritz, France, travelling by bus to Bayonne, France, where I stayed one night and one day.

On April 10th, I left Bayonne and travelled by bus to Saint-Jean-Pied-de-Port. The bus was full of future pilgrims from all around the world. As we got out of the bus and collected our backpacks, one pilgrim told me that my backpack was too heavy.

I smiled; it weighed 13 kg, like when I crossed France and Spain during my first Camino at the age of 64, covering approximately 2,500 km. I thought to myself, some things never change.

Once in Saint-Jean-Pied-de-Port, I looked for my lodging, took possession of my bunk and went to the Pilgrims' Office to register and buy my Credential 'Pilgrims' passport'. What is a Credential? It is a folded document identifying you as a pilgrim. It contains many details: family name, Christian names, nationality, your signature, whether you are doing it on foot, bicycle or on a horse. It will indicate where you start your Camino and it allows the pilgrim to sleep one night in a refuge, shelter, monastery or convent. Every day a stamp is put on your document. In a sort of way, it is like a record of your journey and once you arrive in Santiago de Compostela, you are able to request your 'Compostela': the certificate that proves that you have walked the Camino.

At Saint-Jean-Pied-de-Port, not all the workers at the Pilgrims' Office could speak English and I was happy to be able to help and translate the conversations. I was told a job would be ready for me if I wanted to stay! The person in charge gave me a list of all the places we would go through to arrive in Santiago de Compostela. To my surprise, the list was so much longer than the one I had in 2010 which was only one single A4 sheet and in 2018 there were six pages long, indicating how many Albergues had mushroomed in eight years along the path. On this list, you could find private Albergues with their phone numbers and municipal Albergues, with the number of beds, the cost per night, if there was a kitchen and so on. It also showed which Albergues welcomed cyclists.

It was very cold, and it looked as if rain was on its way. I had, accidently, left my rain-jacket in my school friend Suzanne's car and went to buy a rain-jacket, a pair of trousers for the rain and two trekking posts. As I came out of the shop, I bumped into two Australian pilgrims, Jerry Everard and his wife, Sharon Boggon, who were members of the Camino Group Facebook page in Australia. They had come to my presentation when I talked to the Camino Group in Canberra, in 2015.

It was nice meeting them, we had a chat and separated but not without a hug and a photo. As I was walking in the main street of Saint-Jean-Pied-de-Port, I crossed paths with other pilgrims from around the world. They were lovely encounters.

Back at my lodging, Eric, the owner of the refuge was talking to a young German pilgrim, giving him some advice with profound words of wisdom. From his words I could see that Eric had walked the Camino and lived it to its fullest. This interaction warmed my heart as I was still apprehensive of meeting the group. Later on, I met the two male New-Zealanders members, Mark and Ray. We went for coffee and got acquainted. Tired from the flight, they wanted to have a rest, and I decided to have a walk around the town and climbed up to the top of the hill around Saint-Jean-Pied-de-Port where the view was breathtaking. At the top of the hillock I met a French couple who had visited Australia. Australia was not very far from me, always around the corner: so warming to the heart.

In the evening, I met the other members of the group, Fergus, producer (New-Zealander), Noel Smith, cameraman and producer (Australian), a lovely young English girl, Phoebe, who was going to be the sound technician, and the other members, the two female New-Zealanders' Cheryl and Julie, and the other Australian, Susan. Susan and I had 'met' on the Australian Camino Facebook page that she has created, so many years ago. We were going to be a team of nine.

On 11 April, seven days after my 72nd birthday, as we were leaving the Albergue, Eric said to me that my bag was too heavy. I smiled. We shook hands, and Eric wished me: 'bon chemin - Buen Camino'.

It was a cold and rainy day. It felt like snow was not far away. I did not mind, I was going to start my second Camino. Before the climb of the Pyrenees, walking along the main street in Saint-Jean-Pied-de-Port, a French lady wished me: 'Bon Chemin – Buen Camino'. I felt the magic of the Camino had started and filled my heart.

All the team was booked into Orisson for the night. If you start your Camino from Saint-Jean-Pied-de-Port at 200 metres above sea-level, within eight kilometres you are at 800 metres above sea-level. To me, it is wiser to stop at Orisson. Indeed, from there, you have to walk twenty-one kilometres to reach Roncesvalles with nothing in between. Very soon, the group separated as not all the members were walking at the same pace. I was climbing alone when I crossed paths with a few Scottish and French pilgrims who were going to walk up to Roncesvalles, in one go.

I do not know if I was tired, or if it was because I started from Saint-Jean-Pied-de-Port but I found the climb harder than the first time, or maybe it was because I was older. I kept on climbing with a sturdy pace when suddenly the fog started falling and I caught up with Susan. We walked together for a while, and then we were separated, as we stopped at different times for a breather. Susan asked me to go ahead, I was just a few metres in front of her, walking on the road and missed the path which was on my right and shorter. Susan had called out to me, but I did not hear her and arrived last at the Albergue. Trust me, what a start! I could not change my track record!

My normal daily ritual was going to be: registering on arrival, the hospitaliera or hospitaliero putting a stamp on my credential, taking possession of my allocated bunk, showering, and washing my clothes by hands. My chores finished, I would join the group.

As I arrived at the Orisson refuge, I looked for the owner, Jean-Jacques. I had met him in 2010. I wanted to know if Amar was still coming to the refuge. On 30 May 2010, I had arrived in Orisson, after walking eight weeks across France. What happened? About 500 km, as the crow flies, well before in Saint Jean-Pied-de-Port, somewhere in the 'Pays des Monts d'Ambazac', I had fallen while climbing down a mountain, after I had passed a town named Marsac. Though I had some treatment along the way, when I reached Orisson my knee was still the size of a football and extremely painful. Amar, a Jesuit, and an ex-doctor of the Foreign Legion, had treated my knee.

He had learnt Chinese medicine, and joined the Society of Malta Order of Saint John of Jerusalem (ex-Knights Templar) and was giving his time 'pro bono' to the pilgrims. To this day I am convinced that if I had not met him at Orisson, I would not have been able to finish my first Camino, even with my stubbornness. I was so looking forward to meeting him again and thank him. But, Amar had passed away three weeks previously. I was so saddened by this news. Maybe, when you are not meant to cross paths again with someone, it will never happen.

My lesson was: take any opportunity presented in front of you when it arises, later on it will be too late and you will not be able to.

At Orisson, you are able to enjoy your first experience as a pilgrim, and have an idea what your Camino is going to be. It is an experience not to be missed. Everyone says their name, where they are from and why they are doing the Camino. This is followed by a convivial communal meal. Here, I met Judith from Brisbane who was starting her first Camino.

After a good night's sleep, we went for breakfast and were told that we could not go through the pass as one and a half metres of snow had fallen during the night. A taxi-van had been booked and we were to be driven to Valcarlos.

We crossed forest after forest, in the rain, along wet and muddy paths. It would be quite nice to walk this path later in spring when the trees are covered in leaves. There are little brooks too. It is definitely not as strenuous or difficult as the Napoleon route. However, before reaching Ibaneta pass and its chapel, the ascent is somewhat more challenging. Perhaps we feel that way as all the climbs from Valcarlos are gradual.

It poured rain and I stopped to take off my glasses, I was going to put them in my backpack when a young Spanish pilgrim from Alicante passed by me. She was walking slowly and told me that she was hungry. I had bought a sandwich at Orisson, and gave it to her. We had a bit of a chat and I kept on walking solo. I was nearly close to Ibaneta, when the rain stopped. I decided to wear my glasses again. A huge drama! I could not find them in my backpack. It was impossible for me to read without them.

I panicked, then calmed down and decided to walk back to where I had stopped and given my sandwich to the young Spanish girl. Perhaps they had fallen from my backpack, I did not know. I was half-way down when I met another pilgrim from Austria, Isabella, and asked if by any chance she had seen a pair of glasses on the side of the path. She had and picked them up. I was so relieved. The magic of the Camino was definitely back. I arrived at Roncesvalles, and looked for the Albergue for Pelegrinos. This one was the new Albergue. Well what a change! I was welcomed by gracious Dutch volunteers and directed to where the group was going to stay during the night.

Each floor was divided into alcoves for four or six bunks, I was amazed. The kitchen was huge as well as the bathrooms. It was so big and modern. What a luxurious place to stay! I recalled my last visit when I spent the night in the monastery where I found 124 bunks in the nave with only two showers and toilets for women and two showers and toilets for men. After a chit-chat and a meal with the group, I went back to the 13th century Gothic church dedicated to Saint-James. It is also called 'The pilgrims' Church' and listened to the mass. Julie and Noel came too. Back at the Albergue, Fergus informed Susan and me that we would be walking with the crew the next morning. Wow! Reality sinks in, a bit late to back off. I shrugged my shoulders and went to sleep.

We left Roncesvalles in the direction of Zubiri. We crossed many small villages and it was a strange feeling to walk and put my feet on the same path I walked on so many years ago. We crossed the famous 'sorginaritzaga' forest and many wooded areas, meadows, streams. The path was very, very muddy and treacherous at times. Susan and I could not stop talking and laughing. It is quite easy to forget that what you say is being recorded and filmed. At one stage,

Susan said that we will never arrive in Zubiri, if we do not stop laughing. I have to tell you that every time I laughed, I would stop walking. Susan saw a children's playground and suggested we should go on a swing. At first, I refused, and then agreed. I had just got on the swing when I lost my balance and fell backwards on my 13 kilograms backpack: a hilarious moment.

Later on, Fergus asked me to give him my backpack as he felt it was too heavy for me to carry. I smiled I did not find it too heavy, really. Fergus gave me his backpack, weighing like a feather in comparison to mine. Trust me, I realised that it was very pleasant to walk with a lighter backpack. A while later, I heard a voice, it was Fergus who asked me to take back my backpack as it was killing his back. As usual, I smiled, took my backpack and kept on walking. He asked me what I was carrying in there.

All went well, until I told him that I had been in contact with the writer, Terry McHugh, from Ireland, who wrote about his Camino years earlier. We had decided to bring with us our personal book in the hope we would meet somewhere along the way and exchange them. I have to admit I was eager to meet Terry, another Camino writer. Fergus was quite surprised and kept asking how heavy my book was. At last, I replied: '500 grams'. Fergus was stunned and told me to leave my book somewhere as my bag was already too heavy and I was adding 500 grams.

The night before, I had received a message from Terry McHugh. He had informed me that he nearly lost his life at Espinal, while crossing the Arga River, after the heavy rain of the previous days. The current was so strong and impetuous that he had lost his balance and the water dragged him many metres downstream. He had been lucky as some pilgrims were there and able to pull him out of the water just in time before he was taken further down the river, without any chance of being rescued. After this dramatic incident, he realised how quickly one's life can change and how his family became more important than ever. He was so shaken that he did not know if he would be able to keep on walking the Camino. Fergus and I kept our thoughts to ourselves, not discussing it any further that day.

A few days later, I received another message from Terry saying he had tried so hard to keep on going, but the fear he had experienced in the river, of not been able to see his wife again constantly played on his mind. He has been so scared of losing his life and was missing her and his family so much that he could not finish his Camino. He was returning home to Ireland. I was so touched by his words and the love he had for his wife and family. Love is love.

I had replied by text: 'The Camino will always be there for you another time. When I stop in a big city I will post 'Boots to Bliss' to you, just text me your address and, I will text mine and you can post it. I will get it when I am back in Australia. Take care and all my best wishes to you and your family'.

The signage was still very good. However, we noticed that for the number of kilometres written on the signposts, it was a different matter. The more we walked the kilometres between the same villages were increasing. It was so funny and we joked about it.

At the top of the mount 'Alto de Erro', there is a descent to Zubiri which is precarious especially if it is muddy. I descended it very slowly as I did not want to get hurt. Susan and the crew walked in front and I walked solo. On the way down, I saw a lady pilgrim who was struggling a lot. I asked her if I could be of any help. She shook her head saying: 'No'. I kept climbing down and left her with our friendly 'Buen Camino'. As I was descending the trail, I could not keep her out of my mind and started to feel guilty for letting her go down alone as the path was getting worse and more slippery. She had looked so unsure and unsteady. As I arrived at the entrance of Zubiri, Fergus and Noel were waiting for me, and I shared with them how worried I was for this lady, and told them that I had to go back. If this woman was in trouble, she might not be able to make it before the night. Fergus and Noel dissuaded me. I felt even worse. The guilt of not helping another human being became overwhelming. We reached the 14th century medieval bridge 'Puente de la Rabia' (Rabies Bridge) over the river Arga when Susan arrived in the opposite direction. I told her that if anything happened to this woman, I would never forgive myself. Eventually, the woman arrived accompanied by her husband.

Before going to dinner, Fergus approached me and said: 'Claude, you were so concerned about this woman, do you think, your reactions were due to the fact that you revisited what happened to you in France, at the beginning of your Camino, when you got lost every day and in the forests?' I shrugged my shoulders, looked at him and said: 'No, not at all'.

The whole group went to eat at a little café for our evening meal. The cost of a three course pilgrim meal was 10 Euros. If you are a vegetarian, you have two 'hors d'oeuvres' (first dish), mostly salads, which replaces the main dish. Obviously, this is not sufficient, especially if you have to walk long distances the next day. To compensate, for breakfast, I ate a Spanish omelette with potatoes which was more sustainable for walking so many kilometres on a daily basis.

That night, lying on my bunk, I pondered about Fergus' question. Maybe he had a point. My first Camino started in France at Vezelay, the starting point of Via Lemovencis. For more than 15 days I had not met one single pilgrim along the trail. The signage was very poor and with my bad sense of direction, I got lost almost on a daily basis sometimes in forests, in the countryside. I did get fearful till I learnt to trust myself that all would be okay at the end. One of the lessons I had to learn during my first Camino was: trust, as I have been betrayed so many times during the course of my life. In those days, there was no GPS. I still walk without a guide-book or a GPS. If you are walking in France, I would suggest you take a guide book or a GPS. It is not as necessary if you are walking in Spain.

The next morning, we left Zubiri for Pamplona. Soon I found myself alone as the others were walking faster, and being younger, though some not so much younger than me, it was understandable. It did not bother me at all, I wanted to enjoy my Camino, not getting hurt by walking too fast, wanting to cover every millimetre till the end and finishing it in one piece. This would be a daily recurrence, except when I was walking with the crew. At the end of every day, we would eat together, which was lovely.

Due to the pouring rain the previous days, the river was flowing like a torrent and at times the path was covered by fallen trees or bushes blocking the path. Spring in that area was waking up as well, with the flowers in the fields and on the side of the road blooming with their various spring colours. On the way to the little village of Zabaldika, I met Alexander from the Netherlands.

After a little break at a coffee place and meeting more pilgrims, we started again. There were two paths. Most of the pilgrims kept going along the Camino Way. We decided to take a detour and visit San Esteban (St Stephen) 13th century Chapel at the top of a steep hill. Before the steep hill, there was a cross in remembrance of a lady who finished her Camino, as she died at that spot. Once at the top, it was magical: around the chapel there were some beautiful tulip flower-beds. I thought: 'Alexander would feel right at home here'. The entrance of this church is very impressive with its three Romanesque arches. We were welcomed by a lovely nun, who showed us around. Through a tiny circular stone staircase we reached the top of the tower where we found two bells, one in each arched window.

From there we could see the whole valley below and its surrounding mountains. I rang the smallest one. It is the oldest of the whole of the Navarre region. Its sound was magical and resonated above the valley. I felt my heart sing and I let it fly with the sound of the bell. On the left hand side of the altar there was a wooden carved Christ behind a glass window with hundreds of small pieces of yellow folded papers put there by pilgrims or visitors. They wrote their wishes, dreams, hopes or prayers. I did too. Close to the chapel there is a modern pilgrims' refuge run by the Sisters of the Sacred Heart.

Back on the road, Alexander and I kept on walking, sharing more about ourselves. We met only one pilgrim along that section as we took another detour. The track was quite muddy. We went downhills and uphills, forests, and crossed small villages with their ancient houses with tilted roofs, till we arrived at a medieval bridge over the river Ulzama leading to Trinidad - Arre. I did not visit the church. I had to catch up with the group. We put a stamp on our credentials. Alexander added these touching words beside the stamp:

'Thank you for the lovely day on the Camino. Spread your wisdom and love. Alexander'.

We hugged and separated as Alexander was going to stay at the Monastery, while I was keeping on walking towards Pamplona, the ancient Capital of the Kingdom of Navarre between the 9th and 16th centuries.

As mentioned above, I had asked Fergus, if I could stay in municipal Albergues, but this did not happen with the exception of a few times where we all stayed in them. Indeed, it was too difficult for me to be in one place and the others in another Albergue and it was going to be too tricky to find nine free bunks on arrival every day. So it was decided that we would stay in private Albergues. Phoebe was looking after this logistic and performed that challenging task extremely well.

I re-joined the group at the municipal Albergue 'Jesus Y Maria' which is extremely comfortable. In the late afternoon, we visited Pamplona with its many malls and green areas. The city was packed with people. Some men had been wrongly accused of something and there was a demonstration. Some leaders came and shared their frustration from a podium in the centre of the city. For the members of our group, it was their first experience of how a Spanish crowd can be noisy. I am sure it would be worse for a football match!

After a good night's sleep and breakfast, I was back on the road and, to my surprise, I bumped into Alexander again. We waved, hugged, and each other went our own way. I was trying to find my way out of Pamplona and remembering where I went through eight years before. Our memory can be quite tricky. I had passed the University of Navarra and I was well outside of Pamplona when my body asked me to stop for an urgent matter. I looked and looked and looked, but I could not find any public toilets along that section, nor coffee places. Having no choice, I kept on walking, grumbling about the local governments and wondering why they did not build or put demountable public toilets along the path, as they could create jobs and everyone would be quite happy to be charged one Euro, to use the facilities.

After walking for quite a long time, with no hope in sight of finding a coffee place, I became quite desperate when I saw a man on the porch of his house and asked him where I could find a coffee-bar. He pointed one out to me at the top of a hill. I would find it on the left hand side of the road. As I got close to it, I felt an uncomfortable sensation as if I should not go there, and then I saw that twenty metres further on another coffee place. I listened to my instinct and went there. I ordered a coffee and I was saved! I sat at the terrace to drink my coffee and met Amélie and Claudia from Germany. The niece and aunt were walking together the Camino Frances. I met Kathie who was walking her Camino with her husband, collecting money for a charity she had created. She wanted to use the money collected to take young girls and boys out of prostitution in India. I felt so touched by her story and her dedication. What a beautiful soul! I held her in my arms and she cried on my shoulder. After giving her a hug, I noticed a man looking at us. I went back inside the coffee-bar and I smiled at him as I passed, and we looked at each other. On my way out, I asked him if he wanted a hug too. This is the way I met Gerald from The Netherlands. We hugged. I took my backpack and left.

I was on my way to Zariquiegui, when I met Harrison who was talking about energies and our interactions as humans with nature and our world. I enjoyed our conversation a lot and we walked together for quite a while. Harrison was so much younger than me, and I realised that my pace could not match with his, and so I told him kindly that he could go ahead if he wanted, as I walked slower than him. I thought: no problem with that one, who is not younger than me on this path. He smiled. We hugged and separated, walking each at our own pace. There were more crosses along the path. I was not quite at the top of the hill above Zariquiegui when I saw Harrison waiting. I was somewhat surprised to find him there.

As I got close to him, to my surprise, he told me that he was waiting for me. After our hug, he started to cry uncontrollably, something had happened in his psyche through my hug. I felt so blessed and told him, the Camino does that and his healing process has started. I was so happy for him. We hugged again and he left, not without thanking me.

I replied: 'I have done nothing. There was no coincidence, we were meant to cross paths. I told him to travel well and live the moment, to walk his Camino the way it is meant for him to walk it. I am sure we will meet again'.

As it was cold, I did not find the climb to Alto Pedron difficult and was able to absorb myself in the beauty of the landscape. While climbing, I reflected on the public toilets and my thoughts regarding this matter. In fact, I was totally wrong, and the local governments were pretty clever. Having no public toilets built along the path, the pilgrims have to go to a coffee place and buy a coffee or something else, to use their toilets. Therefore, the owners have to employ more staff and the governments not only reduce unemployment, but collect taxes from the owners and their staff and they do not spend one cent to maintain them. Well, Claude, you were quite wrong and I smiled at myself.

I reached the top of Altro Pedron, with its famous wrought-iron statues; I stopped for the traditional photo, and climbed down the steep hill covered in loose stones and gravel which could be quite an unstable section. I decided to go down in zigzag fashion, to protect my knees. I arrived at Uterga, and then went in the direction of Puerta La Reina, which is an important town as the fourth French route from Arles going through the Somport Pass joins the Camino de Santiago. From then on, the path was called the Camino Frances. The next morning, I started walking with the other members of the group, with the exception of the ones filming; soon, they were well in front. It was going to be like that during the whole Camino. I was not fazed at all. Each one to its own journey!

On my way to Maneru, an 11th century village, I met pilgrims from Sweden, America, and Spain, who told me they had heard about me on the path. I smiled and chatted a bit. I left them after giving them a hug and taking the traditional photo. They were resting there and I had to get to Estella before nightfall. After Maneru, you go through vineyards before reaching the entrance to Cirauqui meaning 'vipers' nest'. The village is perched at the top of a hill and to access it, I ascended the steep narrow, cobbled streets with their medieval houses and coats of arms, with vineyards on each side of its slopes, passing in front of the 11th century Roman church. It was closed, just as it was eight years ago.

I crossed the village of Lorca, over its old Roman Bridge, and then walked along a country road with its green fields.

While going up a little hill, after Lorca, I met, for the second time, Amélie and Claudia from Germany. I walked with Amélie for a while and then with Claudia, walking one by one and at the same pace allowed more sharing. Soon they would stop. During our conversations, I was listening and at the same time, scrutinising the path, looking for two heart-shaped stones. I wanted to gift them in memory of our meeting on the Way, as I felt our paths would never cross again. We hugged, wishing each other a 'Buen Camino'.

Eventually, I arrived at Estella. I was tired and really happy that our lodging was at the entrance to the town, not far from the bridge leading to the centre of the ancient and important city of Estella. When you are walking with a group you start at point A and have to finish at point B, even if you are dead tired. The group was not there and this was quite normal.

The members wanted to visit the various places where we were going to stop. We always shared our evening meal either in a restaurant or as a communal meal, which was nice.

We had decided to go and eat at a restaurant in the town, when I saw, Jennifer, from the Brisbane Camino Group enter. In Brisbane, I had told her that I would stay in municipal aubergues along the Way. Jennifer was a hospitaliera at the municipal Albergue. She had heard that Camino Skies' group was staying in town and was wondering why I had not enrolled. She had found out where we were having dinner and here she was. It was nice to see her again. She was staying a few extra days at the municipal Albergue as a 'hospitaliera' before starting her Camino again, as she had, previously, hurt herself.

There are two ways to reach Los Arcos, and it was decided that we would go through Irache, where there is the famous fountain 'Fuente del Camino'. I took the other path in 2010, via Eurate as I was not interested in this tradition at all. I went to bed as early as I could, leaving the members playing cards, as I knew the next day would take us to Los Arcos, which was going to be a hard day climbing to Villamayor de Monjardin.

As I arrived at the Fountain, I saw Amélie and Claudia pouring some wine into their water bottles. Surprised to see them again, we waved. I kept on walking, passing by the Fountain.

I enjoyed the majestic scenery with its mountains, vineyards, and dirt paths. I appreciated the change. I found it is harder to walk on cobble stone roads and asphalt road than dirt paths. I passed the 12th century Romanesque 'Fuente de Los Moros' (fountains of the Moors). Beware: its water is not drinkable. Well before entering Los Arcos is the Castle Romanesque de Sam Esteban de Deyo.

Amazingly, our group was staying in the same Austrian Albergue I stopped in during my previous Camino. After all my chores, I went downstairs and met Nadine, from France. I was very touched by her story. She was walking for a member of her family and had walked from Le Puy en Velay (France), doing some sections each year.

I went wandering in the town to find out where the path was for the next day, so I could gain a few minutes and not arrive so late, in comparison with the group. On my way back to the refuge I found some members of the group sitting at the terrace of a café having drinks, not far from the Romanesque Church of Santa Maria de Los Arcos.

The next day, I travelled out of Los Arcos quite easily, and then became confused by the signage as there were two different directions. A local was walking his dog and showed me the way and told me one was following the highway, the other passes through some countryside and small villages. I took the scenic path and crossed a number of hills. The path, that day, was mostly on gravel roads and at times with sharp descents. I was crossing what looked like a small forest when I saw a stand selling fruit and drinks. It was a new thing on the path: many little stands had sprung up along the Way. A few metres further I saw Cheryl sitting on the side of the path deep in her thoughts. I sat beside her quietly, waiting for her to open up, as I felt she needed a listening ear. Eventually, she did. After this special time, heart to heart talk, I saw a heart-shaped stone not far from my feet, I picked it up and at the end of our sharing I gave it to her. We left this little paradise and walked together to Viana.

The next morning, I left Viana with Fergus, Noel, Phoebe and the camera. We talked, and I sang French childhood songs, I had learnt at pre-school.

We laughed a lot. On our way to Logrono, I was looking forward to meeting Feliza's daughter, Maria, again, who had followed her mother's tradition since her death. Feliza was well-known on the Camino as she had been the first one to open her house to the pilgrims offering coffee, cakes, drinks or a seat in her house. Sadly Maria had passed away and now her cousin was continuing with the tradition. The energy was different; it had become a kind of business. I was saddened, as in life nothing is permanent. We are born and we die: that is life. There were more crosses for pilgrims who had died along the Way.

We arrived in Logrono, the capital of La Rioja region, where we stopped for a coffee and a break while Fergus went to do some photocopies. After this breather, we kept on walking. Needless to say, we had a good time and joined the others at Navarrete.

The following day, I walked a little while with Julie from the group. I could feel that her heart was heavy. Walking day in and day out, changes arise in our inner self and sometimes pilgrims need to open up. If you meet that person at the right time, you will become their listening ear. It was not yet the time for Julie to share. When the time was right, if she wished, I would be there for her. Everyone grieves differently and we have to respect that, it's the least we can do, even if our heart knows and wants to help.

Later on I met Mark, another member. We had a heart to heart talk; losing a child is so painful. How can anyone understand in the depth of their soul when we have not lived through such a difficult time? After the sharing, Mark told me that he was thankful that I was there for him at that specific time as he needed a listening ear. Mark was a fast walker and went ahead. I hoped: from now on, he would walk with a lighter heart.

I passed a spot where pilgrims had built some small stone monuments. I crossed a lot of vineyards as well as almond groves. At an intersection, I met a shepherd with his flock. He asked me to take his photo, which I did with pleasure. By the way, Spanish almonds are so delicious and wonderful for a quick snack. As I arrived on the outskirts of Najera with its semi-industrial areas, I got lost again. I could not find the bridge I had crossed. It was not indicated clearly and I went through a lot of streets, before someone put me on the right path. Again, I had no GPS or guide-book, and had given the list of villages to cross to a pilgrim in Orisson, as the Way is in principle, so well signed. Maybe I was just too much in my thoughts and therefore not careful enough.

Najera had been a very important point during my first Camino, as from this town, it became more powerful. Events had made me more aware of how to look at coincidences I was encountering.

Being the last one to arrive every day was my daily worry, though no one from the group seemed to be bothered by it. I was the one who was feeling inadequate. I was the oldest, this was a good excuse. Therefore, I did not take the time to return and pray at the monastery of Santa Maria La Real where the Kings of Navarre are buried. After crossing the bridge, I asked a lovely young lady for directions. It was when I was at the back of a huge medieval building, that something very strange happened: tears started to roll down my cheeks. I was shocked. What was going on? Why now and for what reason? I kept on walking, so surprised by this reaction. At the end of the perimeter of that building, I climbed a little hill, saw a coffee place and went in. I asked a waiter what was the name of the building I had just passed a few metres before. It was the back of the Monastery of Santa Maria La Real.

Surprised, I said: 'What! The Monastery of Santa Maria La Real!'

My reaction startled the waiter. With a brief 'thank you', I left shaken. Why such a reaction? What happened in 2010? I had stayed for the night at Najera and went wandering in the town. My feet led me to the Monastery. I went first to the church which was completely empty. I wanted to visit the crypt where a statue from the 13th century of the Virgin Mary with Jesus on her lap was displayed. As I was approaching the entrance to the cave, I felt as if someone was pushing me towards the tombs of the Kings and Queens of Navarre, especially the one of Queen Estefania. It was so strong and powerful; I felt I had to go there first. For some very odd reason, I needed to stroke their hands; I could not control this impulse as well as from the ones of another female tomb. When I left the church, parishioners and pilgrims started to come in. A few days earlier, just after Logrono, I had met Anna-Maria from Switzerland who had performed some reiki on me, as my breathing was so bad. It was the first time I had had reiki. I had met her again at Najera after the episode in the Church and I had asked her to explain to me what had just happened at the Monastery. Anna-Maria had asked me if I believed in reincarnation, to which I replied that I was open to most things, and I believe in life after death. She added that I may have a connection with this place, that I was blessed and so lucky to have that experience.

Now, eight years later, I was passing behind the same monastery, and this happened! Oh dear!

Later on, I was close to a village, when I was stopped by a Spanish man, who asked me if I had some pain in my feet. I smiled and kept on walking.

He said: 'I can see you are suffering, be careful if you want to finish your Camino'.

In fact, I had fallen down on some gravel a few kilometres prior, though the path was easier and my feet had been painful for a while. I had been too much in my thoughts and not looking where I put my feet. Strange things can happen during your Camino, if they are meant to be. I kept on walking towards Azofra. I was the last to arrive again, though I had hoped not to arrive too late.

After a restless night, as there were a lot of pilgrims snoring in the dormitory, I went out and was struck by how cold it was that morning when I left Azofra. The group had already left. Eventually the sun came out and the day warmed up pretty quickly. There were more pilgrims on the path. I reached Ciruena and was surprised to see the village alive, with people walking about. It was a deserted place in 2010. I stopped for a coffee at the golf club. As I was leaving, I saw two ladies on the terrace. I could not imagine myself drinking a coffee outside as it was still too cold for me, when suddenly one of the ladies got up, looked at me and asked me my name. When I told her it was 'Claude', she replied:

'Claude from Boots to Bliss, I thought, I recognized you. I follow you on your Facebook page. I am Lisa from California, USA, this is Denise from France'.

It took me a second to compose myself. I went towards them, and gave them a hug. An American lady knowing me and following me, on my Facebook page, the little Claude from Australia and we bumped into each other in a small village along the Camino Frances! Wow! I was still surprised by such encounter.

Lisa and I walked together while Denise respectfully stayed a few steps behind us to give us privacy. Lisa shared her life. She was a beautiful soul, who like all of us, had experienced challenges in her life, but these challenges had made her look at life quite differently. Her heart was more open to others. I was blessed to have met her and be part of her journey through life for a little while.

After Ciruena, climbing down a little hill, I saw a small piece of paper on the ground. On one side there was a drawing; a shell with the various places you can find along the Way from Saint-Jean-Pied-de-Port and on the other side, the following words:

'One happy pilgrim....

Keep listening each day for the cheers.

Lots of love and hugs

Dave xx'

I crossed Santo Domingo de la Calzada but did not stop, time was going too fast and I had to reach Granon which was built at the top of a hill. The last few kilometres can be quite a killer as your body gets so tired. That section was not specifically difficult, but long. My eyes had been blessed with green fields and colza flowers on both sides of the path, fairly good weather and my heart full with the memories of beautiful meetings and sharing.

The next day, we would leave the Rioja Region and enter the Castile Region at Redecilla del Camino which is the first village of Castille. I started with the group but soon I was behind everyone. With pain in my legs and feet, my pace was slower. I had not shared with everyone my dilemma, probably, due to the way I was raised and my married life: 'Get on with it, keep walking'. At the same time, I wanted to stop at Vilaria de Rioja and greet Acacio and Orietta at their little Albergue who have my book in their library.

I was at Redecilla del Camino when I saw Harrison coming out of a coffee place. We waved at each other and hugged. He whispered in my ear: 'Claude, I was thinking about you and here you are'. We hugged again, and each walked our own way.

A few minutes later I met two French sisters, Marie-Jeanne and Pauline. They had lost their father and were walking the Camino for him. They asked me my name, and I replied, 'Claude'. Their eyes nearly popped out of their sockets, and they started to cry. I held them. I was carrying the same Christian name as their father. It was too much for them. I let them cry on my shoulder. I knew from my volunteering in palliative care, and my first Camino that crying is the beginning of healing. Once more, I was blessed to be at the right time and in the right place to help my fellowmen.

It was quite early when I arrived at Vilaria de Rioja, close to 11.00am, and I was wondering if Acacio and Orietta would be there. The front door was closed; my heart sank, but I decided just the same to knock at their door anyway. Acacio opened it, I introduced myself; and I was welcomed with a lot of cheers. He said that Orietta was cleaning the refuge. He went back in and called out to Orietta. We were so happy to see each other again, took a photo, and said our good-byes. In front of their Albergue there was a lovely sign showing the Way and the number of kilometres to cover before reaching Santiago: 576 km.

Back on the road, I stopped at Beldorado for a coffee where I met two Australian pilgrims Nick and Peta. They told me that pilgrims were talking about me on the path. I was still quite surprised at this news. Well, it must be the 'Radio Pilgrims', a talk around the table during the evening meal, I presumed. I stayed a bit longer than planned. Nick, Peta and I had a deep spiritual conversation about coincidences, why we meet certain people at certain times, during our life, and the increase of racism in the world. They had some members of their family living not too far from Brisbane and we hoped that one day we would meet again when they visited.

It was a lovely stretch walking between green fields, and typical old Spanish villages in between with their churches, and so peaceful. It was perfect as my pace was slower and was in so much pain. I was crossing a river over a bridge when I saw a snake on the embankment in the grass. I arrived near Tosantos and met Veronica. We had met previously in Orisson, nearly 210 km away.

This is the Camino, you met, then each one goes his or her own way, and you meet again. There always seems to be a reason why you meet again. Veronica, a very reserved person, noticed some small changes in herself and she was ready to be more open. For her, it was a huge change. Thanks to the Camino, she had realised that she was stronger than she thought. I was so happy for her. Her approach to life would be different from now on.

After Tosantos, there is a steep stony narrow road to go up before reaching the village of Villambistia. I was very tired, in pain and it was late. The entire group had prepared a communal meal in the kitchen. It was nice to meet and chat without the noise of restaurant patrons. The meal was totally vegan and vegetarian for Phoebe and me. I was touched by their kindness. My bunk was at the top. Mark approached me suggesting we should swap bunks. I was so relieved. My leg was creating mayhem in my body, but I did not want the others to know, and climbing the ladder could have shown that I was in trouble. I heard a beep and checked my phone. I had a problem with my sim card and most of the time it did not work. In principle, this did not bother me. This time it was working. I opened it and saw a message from Alexander with an attachment. In the attachment, there was a drawing with the following words: 'A butterfly Camino Angel on the Camino'. Alexander had drawn this picture after our first meeting. How sweet!

From the village of Villambistia, the path starts with a slightly steep narrow gravel road. Reaching Espinal del Camino, the path is mostly flat with fields on both sides I recognized the ninth century ruins of Santo

Felicies de Oca's old monastery, crossed the river over a somewhat wooden bridge, and with planks nailed on the trunk of a tree. I was not far from Villafranca Montes de Oca, where after the town, a steep track would greet me along with some forests. Walking in the countryside, it was so much easier to remember where I had passed through many years ago than it was in the city, where more buildings had been built.

After the climb and crossing some forests, I saw my first primroses. Spring was arriving. I crossed paths with some pilgrims and we shared the usual: 'Buen Camino'. It was drizzling. At the top of a plateau there was a monument, with a cross where pilgrims had left some items such as a cap, rosaries, ribbon. From there, as far as the eye could see, there was a long dirt stretch between plantations of pines. It was looking eerie as a mist was falling.

In the middle of the path a heart had been designed out of small stones and further on there was an arrow indicating which way to go; ahead. The 'heart' has always been my motto, walking the Camino. Nothing can be done if your heart is not open to others.

Suddenly, in the middle of the forest there were stands. Something new has sprung; Spanish people had set up their little businesses there, with wooden seats and tables so pilgrims could rest. This spot has been named: 'El Oasis del Camino'. The trees have been transformed into totem. What a change in eight years! I bought some boiled eggs and enjoyed a warm coffee. There was a dog, but it was well domesticated and was staying not too far from its owner.

Close to San Juan de Ortega, I met Owen, a young German man. He was walking the Camino hoping to find who he was and which direction he should take for his future life. Nowadays, many young people are wondering about their future and the direction of the world. Many do not fit in it with its focus on money, selfishness and loss of community. They have been to university, studied very hard as they thought that was the way to walk their path, or please their parents, till once in the world they realise that it is not their passion.

In Europe, many young adults take the Camino to find out who they are, away from their environment. I wished him well and we left.

Following a gravel road, I passed the 12th century Gothic church of San Juan de Ortega. San Juan de Ortega had dedicated his life to pilgrims and built this church. Leaving San Juan de Ortega, I took a forest path then I went over a beautiful meadow where some cows and their calves were grazing. I went to pat them, and they did not move. I also saw as well two labyrinth circles drawn probably by pilgrims, in the middle of the field. Soon I arrived at the entrance of Ages with its beautiful tulip flower beds welcoming me and re-joined the group.

The next morning, I left the old village of Ages, in a light rain and mist; the others were already on the road. The rain and the mist were going to be my companions for most of the day till I reached the outskirts of Burgos.

Before Burgos there is the village of Atapuerca where some remains from a million years ago were found. It is said to be the site of the first Europeans. Leaving Atapuerca, I crossed a forest, and then the path is uphill, I may say increasingly steep and stony or should I say rocky until I reached The Termino de Atapuerca. There I met Owen again and he shared more. This second meeting was meant to be and necessary for him to go forward in his life. It was nice to see him again. I felt blessed to be there for him at that special place. Roland and Clarisse from Germany arrived and told me that they had heard so much about the 'Little Claude from Australia' and were thrilled to have had the opportunity to meet me. I felt I was the one who was privileged. We all hugged and I waved them good-bye. I love talking to young ones, they warm my heart.

We know what goes up has to go down. Passing the hilltop, well, that stretch was going downhill. It is steep and stony till you come to a gravel road. I crossed villages; on one of the walls there was a funny painting of a pilgrim crushed under the heavy weight of his backpack, I smiled wondering if the designer had seen me in one of his/her dreams, well not quite as the painting represented a man and on the top in a bulb the man slumped in an armchair.

Between the villages of Cradenuela and Orbaneja de Riopico I saw a man digging his garden. It was so well maintained that he reminded me of my Papa, who was the happiest man in the world when he was in his garden and so proud keeping it well maintained with not a blade of grass or weed in site. Towards the end of his life, my Papa could not attend to it anymore, to his despair. I approached the man and congratulated him on his garden. He asked me to come in, showed me around his hens and roosters. His garden was his pride and joy, just like my Papa. At the bottom of his garden, he had a creek, so water was no problem. I left him, he wished me: 'Buen Camino'.

I crossed a bridge and a highway and I came to a point where I had to choose which route I would take. I could not see myself walking along the industrial area so I turned left and took the alternative route along the river. The path is not easy to find after leaving the highway. An elderly Spanish cyclist who was resting on the pavement gave me the direction to follow. The first part of that section is not very nice as you see the back of the industrial buildings, till you reach the river. At an intersection, the cyclist reappeared. He wanted to make sure I was taking the right path as there was no signage. Once I reached the river, walking along it was so beautiful and peaceful, the grass was so green. On each side of the dirt path there was an alley of tall trees. I loved it. I was lost in my thoughts when I recognised Lisa, the American lady I had met at Ciruena who was in front of me. She was walking very slowly as she was suffering a lot. I approached her, we hugged. She told me to keep on going as she was in pain and walking slowly. She found the Camino hard to walk day in day and out, but she would be alright. I did not want to leave her. No way, I did not want to hear about it and stayed with her. Slowly and eventually, we arrived at Burgos in front of the Cathedral. I asked her if she had a lodging, 'no' was her answer. I asked her to sit on a bench:

'Lisa, you are very tired. Let me find a bed for you. You sit here I will find you one for you. You can trust me, I will return. Just promise me that you will not move from this bench, until I return. Promise, Lisa, please, promise'.

She did promise and I left her to look for a place where she could stay. I went to the Albergue I had stayed at in 2010. It is a small Albergue, with only a few bunks, showers, toilets, no kitchen, nothing else. This Albergue was not far from the Cathedral. To reach the dormitory, you have to climb a spiral staircase which is above a church. I was welcomed by a very happy and smiling Spanish hospitaliero. There was one bunk left which he showed me. I was startled as it was the one I had used so many years ago. I asked him to keep it for Lisa. I went back to her as fast as I could. I was so relieved that Lisa had a bunk for the night. We both walked back to the lodging and I left.

It was time for me to look for my lodging which was on the other side of the river. I crossed a bridge, when a group of women passed in front of me. Among them, I saw a familiar face. I must be seeing double, I said to myself. It can't be, and I kept on walking. Troubled, I had to walk back and make sure I was not seeing double. I caught up with the group. I was right. Among the women there was a familiar face, Anna, from the Brisbane Camino group to which I was a member. She had no idea I was walking the Camino, and I had no idea that she was as well. This is the Camino with its surprises.

As soon I was at the lodging, Noel told me that I was coming with them for a small interview in front of the Cathedral. The interview was not even finished when my eyes caught someone I knew, Harrison. It was hard to concentrate as I could see there were more pilgrims I had met along the way and wanted to give me a hug. When I met Harrison for the first time, outside of Pamplona, he had told me that he and his wife would meet in Burgos to walk some part of the Camino together. I had replied that I hoped to meet her and that maybe we might meet in Burgos.

And here she was with Harrison. Maybe hard to believe, but this is the Camino, nothing should surprise you. I gave her a hug, and in my ear, she whispered:

'Thank you, Claude, God blesses you'.

I replied: 'All is well, my dear, it was meant to be. Have a good life and be happy'.

Back at our lodging, I went to buy some food with Fergus and Noel. What a day!

The next day, a cold, windy and misty morning was waiting for us. As always getting out of a big city is challenging. Maybe I took the wrong path, I did not know, and did not care and for a while walked along a park, then I crossed it and amazingly I found my way. That day was my first day on the high plateau called Meseta dreaded by many pilgrims who avoided it and take either the bus or the train to recommence at another point on the Camino Frances. The Meseta starts a few kilometres outside of Burgos, from the village of Rabe de las Calzadas, and finishes at Astorga. It is a long stretch of nearly flat open space 250 kilometres long, with some uphill and downhill and wheat fields on both sides of the path.

It is remote, with long distances between villages; you need to carry enough water, especially if you walk it in summer.

For some, the Meseta is a drudge. Yes, it is hard, not physically but emotionally, walking along flat stretches which can be hard and boring, as you have nothing to distract your mind. To me, it is an opportunity for soul searching and an opportunity for going deeper in our soul so we can start to let go of our burdens. It is said that some lose their mind along the Meseta. It can be true as we all have a story. If your life story is sad, on the Meseta, you won't be able to escape. For me, it is the time for us to learn to revisit the dark side of our life, to learn to let go and then start the process which is going to free you, forgiveness. The Meseta is there to allow you to free yourself and consequently you will forgive others which in return will free you. Do not miss it; embrace it, even if it is hard to let go of your emotional and mental baggage. It is an opportunity not to be missed. Do not be discouraged.

I was at the entrance of Rabe de Las Calzadas when I saw a familiar face a few metres in front of me. It was Lisa. She was feeling better after a good night's sleep and happy to be back on the Camino. I felt she needed to walk alone and we separated. I met two German pilgrims on that stretch, a mother and daughter and a man who was living on the Camino. He could not fit into the world after his first Camino and so he had decided to live on the Camino. Later on, I caught up with the group at Hornillos del Camino.

At the end of our dinner, I was informed that I would be walking the next day with the crew, Mark and Susan and we would be finishing the day at Castrojeric. We left Hornillos del Camino in the dark and, like the previous morning, it was very cold and windy. Later on the weather lifted and it was not so bad. As we were leaving our lodging, I saw a man sleeping on the pavement. I had no idea if he was a pilgrim or a homeless person. Sleeping outside in such cold weather touched my heart and I wondered how many people would have been in that position in the world, that night.

At the end of the village, the path is gravelly and ascends gradually, and then we go through a valley before reaching the village of Hontanas. At an intersection, and well before Hontanas, I noticed a huge pile of stones with four crosses. I was wondering about the significance and walked around it while Fergus found a spot for a good reception for his phone. At the back of this pile of stones there were more crosses. It was a mystery!

As you interact with others and exchange ideas or points of view, you forget pretty quickly that the camera is following you and what you say is recorded. We walked and talked. Even participating in the conversations, I could sense Mark was sad. Mark had lost his daughter and I was praying that the Meseta would be able to help him heal a bit.

Mark, Susan, the crew and I stopped at Hontanas for a coffee break and a bite to eat. We were sitting at a table at the terrace waiting for our order to be delivered when I took the opportunity to talk to Mark on a more personal level. On the path, I saw two heart-shaped stones and had picked them up. A few days earlier Mark and I had a one on one talk. I had told him about a story from 1108 of a sinful Frenchman who had decided to marry and have a family, but he could not have a child and thought it was because of the sinful life he had led and so decided to take the Saint James' Way from his home in France and implored Saint James to help him. Eventually, his wife gave birth to a son, named James. When his son reached the age of 15, the family left France for Santiago de Compostela. As they arrived at the Montes de Oca, James became unwell and died. The mother begged Saint James to return her son to her. At the burial, the young man got up and they kept on walking to Santiago de Compostela, just as the saint had asked them. It was a miracle and maybe this legend teaches us to have faith.

I told Mark my version of this event. It was to show us that there is life after death, to learn, to trust, and to have faith. I gave him the two heart-shaped stones that I had picked up for him one was much bigger than the other one. The heavier representing the way his heart was at the present time and the other one was very light. I was hoping from the bottom of my heart that, in time, he would release his pain and heal as well as being aware of the signs coming to him while he was walking his Camino, so he could find inner peace and finish his Camino with a lighter heart.

Along the straight section towards Hontanas, Susan had a sort of breakdown. I was walking in front of her which was quite unusual. Susan is of small stature and has health issues but she is a fast walker. I turned my head to see where she was when I noticed that she was sitting on the side of the road, her head in her hands. I walked back to help her and finish the walk together.

We arrived at the 12th century San Anton's Monastery, and stopped for a breather. Nowadays you can find coffee shops in front of the Monastery. In 2010, there was nothing there. San Anton's Monastery was a hospital founded in 1146 by the Order of San Antony and the monks used to give a 'Tau' to the pilgrims, which is a small cross as a symbol of protection. In the 21st century, the pilgrims can still stay in the ruins of the Monastery; it is run by the Franciscan Brothers.

From afar, on a mount, you can see the ruins of the castle built by the Templars; it dominated the town of Castrojeriz, the final point of our day. I took a quick shower as I wanted to walk to the top of the castle. There were two steep paths to reach it. Well, I did not make it to the top. The pain under my feet was killing me. I still had many kilometres to walk to Santiago. Sadly, I walked back. Was I becoming wise or wiser? Later, I wandered in the streets and bought what food I needed for the next day. The next day was very important for me, as we were passing in front of a little church called Ermita de San Nicolas and I wanted to stop there.

I was up at the crack of dawn, and left before everybody. Why was I in so much of a hurry? Was it because I knew that I was going to climb a steep hill, a killer for the calves before reaching the Alto de Mostelares? This has an altitude of 900 metres and at the top you can see the beautiful plain with its green fields. Or, was I in a hurry because once I reached a medieval bridge and crossed over the Rio Odrilla I had to descend another challenging steep hill? No, it was for something much more important and special.

In 2010, I had stopped for the night at the little church of Ermita de San Nicolas, which was founded in 1171 and was used as a hospital for pilgrims. At the present time, it is run by the Confraternita di San Jacopo di Compostella of Perugia in Italy. They had only eight bunks. It is a very mystical place; there is no water or electricity in the church, where the pilgrims eat and sleep, but behind it, there is a little building with showers and toilets. I was not sure that the doors of this little church would be open the whole day. Simon Reeve, film maker, had visited here and talked about this little church in his documentary about 'Pilgrimages'. Simon Reeve shared that he was an atheist, but he felt something very special in this church, like an incredible energy. This experience shook him at the time. This documentary was screened in Australia in 2013 on SBS – Australian television.

So why did I want so much to go back there? What happened that I needed to return? Well, during my first Camino, in 2010, I had stopped at Burgos and my feet led me to a Christian shop where I bought two crosses, one for my 'Maman' and one for my 'Papa'. I knew from a strange reason at the bottom of my heart that I had to deposit them somewhere along the Camino Frances, but I did not know where or when. After our candlelight meal, we had mass and afterwards magic happened. We were asked to remove our boots and socks and the two hospitalieros washed our feet. It was done with such gentleness, so much love, that my heart was wide open. It was such a moment of love for all the human beings that I decided to leave the two crosses there. The priest and, the pilgrims blessed them and they were left on the altar. In 2010, 2011, 2012, 2014, 2015, French and Australian pilgrims saw the crosses still there on the altar. I wanted to see if I would see and hold them again, one last time.

As I arrived, the doors were open and I entered. I ran to the altar, but I could not see them. I started to look frantically around the church, looking in every corner, once, twice, three times without any luck. The hospitaliera who noticed me asked me what I was looking for. I gave her my explanation. She kindly looked in the drawers and once more with me around the little church. The crosses were nowhere to be seen; they had been removed. Though I understood that they could not have been kept forever, my heart was heavy. I just hoped that they were placed somewhere safe as I had left there a part of my soul.

Noel and Fergus arrived with the camera, and I was interviewed. It was a sad moment for me, though I was very grateful to the Confraternity to have kept them on the Altar for so long. When things are meant to be, they will be. In this little church, I was closing a chapter in my life.

I left and walked alone most of the way to Fromista. Along that long mostly flat stretch, I met only Peter from Ireland. On one of the milestones someone had written: 'you are divine'. Yes, we are all divine. Sometimes things fall into place, sometimes they do not. We should not despair, just let the day go by in the best possible way we can and accept feeling low. Maybe the message is to be kind to yourself.

When I arrived at the lodging, I found a present from Cheryl on the top of my bunk. Cheryl had bought it at San Anton, the day before. It was a symbol of the Path of Saint James 'a red arrow' painted on a piece of wood. What timing! I thanked and hugged her. This little symbol healed my heart. This little red arrow gave me the following message: look straight ahead and keep on walking your life journey. After dinner, we were asked what would we do if we received millions of dollars, my response was very simple: help the homeless.

Things can go right; things can go wrong in anyone's life. We all hope that it won't happen to us, but who knows, and who is to say that we cannot be in the same predicament, one day, as the homeless. When you walk the Camino day in day out, in any type of weather, you can relate to them and feel for them, even though we have a bunk and a roof above our heads every night: another lesson to learn on the Camino.

I told Fergus that I wanted to take another path the next morning: it was an alternative route. It went through Villovieco. He had no objection and I was grateful. I wanted to return to the section where I healed and released my pain, so many years ago.

Indeed, I threw in the river the little stone Ulf, from Sweden, had given me during my first Camino. We had met, for the first time in Saint Jean-Pied-de-Port as Ulf was starting his Camino from there. He had shared his life story with me and the reasons he was walking the Camino. At the end of our conversation, I had given him a heart-shaped stone. Further into the walk, we met again, that is to say more than three hundred kilometres later at Hornillos del Camino. There, it was my time to open up to him and through our exchanges we had helped each other at a different time. Before Hontanas, Ulf gave me a little stone to throw away when I was ready to release my emotional pain. This is what the Camino is all about. It is a safe place where you can release your pain and start the healing process, if you are ready to do so. You have to be honest with yourself and face your life right in the eye with all the good and the bad things you have done, as well what people have done to you. Ulf returned to the Camino Frances, a year or so later to finish it at Finisterre carrying all the way the little heart-shaped stone that I had given him previously.

I reached the stream and followed it. It was a different time of year; I could not find the same magic.

There were no red poppies, blue cornflowers, yellow buttercups or thistles and the trees looked like ghosts without their green leaves, and even the colour of the water looked different. As we know things are not permanent in life and I kept on walking, trying to find the same magic, to no avail. I saw a small heart-shaped stone along the path and picked it up for Julie, a member of the group, so I could give it to her. Julie had tragically lost her husband and son, and I hoped that this little heart-shaped stone would help her to heal, a bit at least. Sadly, I lost it.

I came to a little intersection and heard some music coming from far away. I decided to follow the sound which led me to a coffee shop and restaurant. In front, there were donkeys grazing, geese wandering in the fields, and a few tepees had been erected. My curiosity got the better of me; I went in and had a coffee. There I met an elderly Italian pilgrim couple, Teresa and Leonardo. They opened up to me and shared their life story. I was so touched by the incredible love they had for each other, though life had not been kind to them. They left and we hugged. Pilgrims had left messages on the walls of the café, as well as photos. I pinned one Camino Skies' flyer like I did previously at various places and I asked the owners if I could write something as well, I wrote:

'On the Camino leave your sorrows and heal' - Boots to Bliss – Claude Tranchant

I was leaving when Julie and Cheryl and the crew entered the café. They had taken the Villarmentero path, and I stayed with them for a while, till we separated, not before showing Julie the message I left there, hoping that she will understand it and find peace when the time would be right for her.

I walked back via the alternative route. I was still hoping to find some of the magic along the rest of the path that I had felt so long ago. It was not meant to be as six male Spanish pilgrims were on the path speaking so loudly that there was no chance for me to meditate, or walk quietly. I walked slower, and then faster, to no avail. In the quietness of the path their voices resonated so far away, in the silence of nature. At the end of that stretch, there were a few dandelion flowers in the field. A little white butterfly, like a little angel, landed on one of the flowers. I smiled, the magic was back.

On my way to Carrion des Condes, I caught up with Teresa and Leonardo who had taken the Villarmentero path, which was shorter than the alternative route, called variant. While I was walking along the alternative route, I was thinking about them, and their life story, when I saw a small stone with two hearts intertwined. I had picked it up hoping to meet them again and here they were. I gave it to them and told them how their story had touched my heart.

They said: 'Claude, we have walked five pilgrimages, but never have we met someone like you. We felt so much love coming out of you; we have never felt something like that before. Thank you for what you gave us, on this section of the Camino'.

Hearing these beautiful words, I started crying. The three of us hugged each other. Their words carried me to Carrion des Condes and filled my heart. I had given so little, I had been their listening ear. To me, I had received much more from them and their life story. I had been the one who had been blessed. We never saw each other again.

I was looking for the Albergue where we were staying when someone called my name: they were the members of the group sitting at the terrace of a café. There had been a change; we were staying at a different address. My French sim card did not work everywhere. I was lucky, once more; I could have been going around Carrion de Los Condes for many hours before finding them. Ha, ha. As usual, being the last one, I went to do my chores and look after my feet. It was then time to have dinner. In the evening in the dining room, Noel and I were having a conversation, when 'a déjà vu' came to my mind. I told him as I was so shocked.

I did not sleep very well that night, more disturbed by the snoring and people coming and going the whole night long and left Carrion des Condes on a very windy day. The rain was so cold. I did not cross paths with many pilgrims that day. In a way, it was a windfall after the emotional day I had experienced the day before. I met some pilgrims who were wrapped up like they were living in Alaska, and I was one of them. It was a pretty flat gravelly section. I was very happy to arrive at Ledigos. It was so cold; it felt like I had walked the whole day in an ice-box.

The next day, I left Ledigos under a cold and gloomy sky. I took the wrong path, till someone called out to me and put me on the right one. Some snowflakes, then hail were my companions for a little while. From afar, I could see the top of the surrounding mountains covered with snow, and this was not something to invigorate me. The Meseta is so flat that you cannot escape the wind, which goes through your bones. Needless to say, the pilgrims were few and far between and it was so cold that no one would have felt like chatting I kept on walking, walking, walking, and walking on the gravel path. My feet and soles were hurting so much. Eight of my toenails had gone dark blue and green; from my previous experience, I knew I would lose them soon. Thinking about pain, how strange does our mind work? It seems that walking alone, the pain is worse, as without any distractions we seem to focus more on our pain. While walking with someone you are so busy chatting or listening that the level of pain seems less. It is the same for the distance you cover, alone, the stretch seems never ending. Walking along any Camino, you reflect a lot and many pilgrims open up to others, healing their heart bit by bit.

Alone and cold, my thoughts flew to my Maman and my Papa, to the pain I gave them when I left France with my little family to migrate to Australia. How my father did everything he could to stop me, but I did not listen. I carried the guilt of giving them so much pain. I never told them that I did not want to go. I did it out of love. Australia had been extremely good to me, and my family. I discovered over the years that I had to come to Australia, to learn and grow, to have a broader understanding of life away from them, where I was so much protected.

As I believe in life after death, I know they have forgiven me, as they would know, now, I had to live in Australia, it was written in the stars. I was sure that from above they were happy and they would keep protecting me, and my little family, maybe as well as pushing me along my path. During all my childhood and youth, they had taught me to be resilient and not to give up. Their life had not been an easy one, born just before and during World War I and living and surviving during World War II. Thank you Maman, Papa, I love you so much.

I reached the half-way mark of the Camino Frances. It was still bitterly cold, and there was still no one on the horizon. One foot in front of the other and in the rain, I found my way to Sahagun. I stopped at the Albergue 'La Trinidad' connected to the Benedictine Order of Cluny in France, so I could have some respite and warmth. A few minutes later, two Australian pilgrims, Jen and Brett arrived, who were walking the Camino:

'Claude, is that you? We recognised you. You came and talked to the Canberra Camino Group, at the Spanish Centre. We were there. We loved your presentation. You are such an inspiration!' Coincidence!

No, we had to cross paths as well as Marline, a French lady, and Petro, an Italian man, who they had met on the Camino Frances a year or so ago. They had returned on the Camino to celebrate their honeymoon, the place where they fell in love. What a beautiful ending!

As I got out of the Albergue 'Trinidad', I met Noel with his friend, the camera. I admired him walking with this heavy equipment.

Along a flat, gravelly long stretch, I saw the famous landmark, shown on many sites:

'Santiago 315 kms –the yellow arrow - Ulteria – plus'. Not far to go!

It had been a long day, a long section, maybe close to 30 kilometres; I was so tired when I knocked at the door of the Albergue. My bunk was at the top, and below me there was a young French girl, about 20 years old and I asked her if she would not mind swapping. A firm 'No' was her reply. I smiled and I replied: 'No problem, I just hope that I won't wake you up if I have to come down during the night.' There was no ladder, as such, just one bar between the bunks at the top and the bottom.

After doing my chores, most of the group were on their bunks trying to keep warm, when I noticed that Cheryl was not there. Nobody knew where she was. I decided to have a look around, when I met the owner who told me where she was. I went to the café; Cheryl was not feeling well. I stayed with her. She needed a listening ear. I was so blessed as I could help her again.

After a good night's sleep, we left Berciamo del Camino for Reliegos. It was still very cold. There was a big plus, the sky was blue, the sun was out, not warm enough though. Along the Camino and the Meseta you see a lot of crosses and that day was no exception. What a beautiful way to leave this earth, doing what you want to do! I was observing the landscape and the mountains when I met Alexandra. She was devastated as she had just received the news that her cousin had passed away. We saw a bench, and talked about him. I tried to find comforting words to ease her pain and urged her to keep on walking her Camino for him and that he would be walking with her. We started walking again and met two young Italians, Sandro and Luciano, selling coffee, fruit and doing massages at the back of their van. Needless to say, I was quite surprised. They were living on the Camino. We bought some coffee and fruit. Then Sandro and Luciano took their musical instruments, and sang and played for Alexandra and me. It was a very emotional moment for Alexandra. Back on the road, I reached Reliegos.

The group was staying at the same Albergue where I stayed eight years prior. Later on, we met at the terrace of a café restaurant where we had our evening meal. The members of the group were starting to feel tired, and it was decided that we would stop for one day at Leon. I told them, that my body does not like to stop and asked if they did not mind if I kept on walking, but covering half of the distance each day so we would meet again at Villa de Mazariffe, which is an alternative route. The members had planned to stay in a hotel. I did not and stayed at the Benedictine Monastery. No one minded and all was well. It was the first time that I had the joy of eating lentil soup since the beginning of my Camino, being a vegetarian, and this soup was a real blessing. In 2010, I could find a lot of lentil or garlic soups. Sadly, in 2018 they had all disappeared from the Pilgrim's menu. If you are a vegetarian and choose the Pilgrim's menu, you will have two hors d'oeuvres which are salads, not enough when you walk a minimum of 20 to 25 kilometres a day, especially in cold weather.

The previous day, I had rung my daughter, Sabine, without success and she had tried to call me back. I did not hear my mobile ringing. It was night time in Australia. I was sad to have missed her phone call.

It was another gloomy and cold day, and I was hoping that somehow the sun would come out at some stage and it did. On my way to Leon, I stopped at Mansilla de las Mullas, where I met, to my surprise, four members of the group who were leaving after having their breakfast. I approached the owner of the café and asked him if he still has his 'Livre d'Or' where pilgrims could write their passage, and I wrote something on it.

Every day, before leaving the shelter, I wrapped each toe with some 'Fixomull stretch' plus some gel toe sleeves, making sure that I closed my boots with the 'Surgeon's Knot'. It helped but not totally. Maybe it was the way I was walking and took it in my stride. That section was a mix of gravel, asphalt roads and crossing the river on a wooden bridge, up and down. I crossed paths with some pilgrims we greeted each other with the traditional 'Ulteria' or 'Buen Camino'- (Good Way).

When I feel that someone does not want to interact, I always respect that and keep on walking. Interrupting is not only rude, but maybe the pilgrim had come to a point of revisiting his or her life and needed to be alone to let go, or just wanted to be alone. Another reason is that when you are exhausted, you do not want to waste your energy talking to someone.

At Arcahueja, I stopped at the little fountain where the words 'Santiago 307 kilometres' were engraved. Did I see two days ago 'Santiago 315 kilometres' before Berciamo del Camino? Hum! I smiled. You can never trust the number of kilometres on a landmark though my feet, my body and my brain remembered walking between these two points and trust, me it is more than eight kilometres!!! We were walking an average of 20 - 25 kilometres daily.

I was not looking forward to walking along the highway to reach Leon. When I arrived at the metal bridge it was closed for repair, the sign indicated to take an alternative route. This change allowed me to cross some quaint villages, away from the busy main roads. I loved it. At the top of a hill, I could see, far below, the city of Leon. This section descending to Leon was steep and slippery, therefore I had to concentrate and climb not straight down but in zigzag fashion again to protect my knees.

I met no one, till I reached Leon and found my way to the Benedictine Convent 'Santa Maria de Carbajal'. Nothing had changed much at the Albergue, with the exception that I had to register at the top of a staircase instead of at the entrance. I was welcomed by a very friendly and smiling hospiteliero: Francisco. I was quite surprised by the numbers of pilgrims already there as I had not met many along the Way that day. In this Albergue, women and men do not sleep in the same dormitory, even married couples. All the bunks in the women's dormitory were occupied. I was surprised as, in 2010, more men walked the Camino Frances therefore they had more dormitories for them than for women.

Consequently there was a change occurring on the Camino Frances nowadays. Francisco went and talked to the management, and they decided to open an empty dormitory for the women to use. After doing my chores, as I did not have any commitment towards the other members of Camino Skies, I wanted to post my book, 'Boots to Bliss', to Terry Mc Hugh as I had promised him. I went back to the office and asked where I could find a post office. Francisco was there and asked the other hospitaliero if he could take a little break and walk me to the post office. Needless to say, I was very grateful. Francisco informed me that I would have to find my way back 'no problem' was my reply. I was appreciative of his kindness.

If you have not been in a Spanish Post Office, it can be quite overwhelming. As I have some knowledge of Italian, I can sort of read Spanish. I had to take a ticket, and checked on a screen when it was my turn, then fill in a form, and buy a box to put the book in and so on. I was filling in the form when I received a message from Terry saying that he was right now at his Post Office and was mailing me his book: 'I have walked 500 miles'. I smiled. Was it a coincidence? No, I did not think so. Terry did not want to send me the book he had carried for me during his short Camino as it has been damaged when his backpack got wet when he fell in the river. I had written back to him saying that I did not want any other copy than this one. It has a story. I was hoping, he would respect my wish and he did. When I arrived back in Australia, his book was waiting for me and I enjoyed reading it very much.

After leaving the Post Office, I walked around Leon, and re-visited the Santa Maria Cathedral, called the 'House of Light', built in the French Gothic style of the 13th and 14th centuries. There was some sort of festival taking place and some very young children were dancing to the sound of Spanish music. My thoughts flew to my grandchildren. I did not come across any member of the group and returned to the Benedictine convent where I bumped into Francoise from France.

Her bunk was not far from mine. Being able to speak your native language is absolutely magical. Francoise and I connected, and enjoyed each other's company. At dinner, we all ate together in the refectory, and we heard a very young pilgrim, Andreas, say that I was glowing. How lovely was that? I thanked him and gave him a big smile.

Andreas was right. I am very happy on the Camino. I leave the world with its problems behind me, but keep my children, grand-children, my family, very close to my heart and mind. After our evening meal in the refectory, we went to Mass.

The next morning, I went to the refectory for breakfast, with all the pilgrims young and old sharing what they had. Francoise was already there, and she asked me if we could have a little chat before leaving the convent. Yes, sure, no problem was my reply.

I met her in the yard. In her hands, she had a necklace and a medal and said: 'Claude, in Carrion Des Condes, the nuns gave me this necklace and medal. I feel I should give it to you. It is more appropriate for you than for me'. I did not want to take it, but Francoise insisted.

Once I had the necklace in my hand, I looked at the medal. I could not believe it. It was the Miraculous Medal! It was unbelievable. My Maman had sent me this medal in the 1980s and I had discovered after her death that she was a devotee of Saint Catherine Laboure, to whom the Virgin Mary appeared on 27 November 1830 and told her to have a medal made according to a certain model. After many conversions and healings had occurred this medal became known as the 'Miraculous Medal'. During my first Camino,

I had worn this medal sent to me by my Maman so many years ago. It has been my constant physical companion. This medal is very important for me; I gave it to my boss who had cancer when I worked at the fruit-shop where I was a check out chick (console operator). He wore it during his cancer treatments and gave it back to me before leaving for my first Camino.

Also, I was descending a mountain, in France, at the Monts d'Ambazac, I had fallen down and hurt my leg. A friend of mine, Dominique from Australia, she had contacted two friends of hers, Cristele and Bruno, who lived in France and asked them to stop me so they could look after me at their place for a while. They were living two or three hours' drive from where I was walking at that time. I had met these two angels along the Way at Saint Foye La Grande. Dominique, knowing me, was certain that I would never stop. After two days' rest, I wanted to leave and be back on the road when Bruno placed something on my leg and had told me to remove it only once my leg was healed. I had reached Najera, in Spain, when I decided to remove it. To my surprise, it was the Miraculous Medal.

Francoise placed the necklace around my neck; she did not have any knowledge about my connection with this medal. Before departing, I told her these stories, we hugged; I felt the hands of an angel passing by. I thanked Francoise. During my first Camino, I had been so blessed and here I was again. I left the convent and disappeared among the crowd.

I was so much in my thoughts, that I got lost crossing Leon. I was not too worried as I had plenty of time. I was going to Virgen Del Camino about eight kilometres from Leon. I asked a Spanish woman, for directions, but she could not understand me. She was accompanied by her grand-daughter, who was about eight or nine years old. Maria was studying English.

With her grand-mother's help, as she was translating our conversation, I was shown the right direction. It is so important to teach children a second language. Maria's little face lit up, so proud of being the translator in front of her delighted grand-mother who could not stop smiling.

For sure, this little interaction would be the main subject at school and at the meal table for the whole family to hear. I hugged her and gave her a kiss. Her grandmother sent me a kiss and said: 'Buen Camino'.

You could not have a better start to the day.

Outside Leon, the endless N120 highway never seemed to finish. I had to cross over a metal bridge. I was not quite at the top of the bridge, when I saw an elderly Spanish lady having difficulty climbing it. I approached her and gave her my arm that she kindly took and we kept on walking slowly but surely. She started to talk to me in Spanish. I could not understand much of what she was saying, but it was not important to me. She kept talking; till we reached a street and she said that her house was in the street on our left. It is at that time that she realised that I was not Spanish, that I could barely speak Spanish. She looked at me deeply into my eyes, kissed my hands and said:

'You have such a gentle face and you are a gentle soul, Carina'.

We hugged and departed, not before I saw she was crossing her little street safely. The strangest thing was that something similar had happened to me at the same spot eight years before or maybe I dreamt this special event.

The direction to Virgen del Camino had changed, and I did not have to walk all the way along the N120, which was quite a relief. I walked along small streets of quaint Spanish houses. I arrived too early at the municipal Albergue and went for a walk around Virgen del Camino, bought some food and visited the contemporary sanctuary of Virgen del Camino's church, built on an old 17th century church, and designed in 1961 by a Dominican Portuguese monk, Francisco Coello. On its façade there are 13 metal sculptures. As you enter, you feel a strong sense of calm and peace, and inside you will find a 15th century statue of the Virgin Mary holding the dead body of Christ.

I returned to the municipal Albergue and met, a young German pilgrim, Xavier. He lived close to the French and German boundaries. Xavier had walked three Caminos with his Mum. We were waiting outside for the Albergue to open, at 16.00 o'clock (4.00pm). Xavier and I talked on many spiritual subjects and the changes which can happen to any human being after walking the Camino. I was so happy to have decided to keep on walking and not stop one day in Leon. I learnt in the last part of my life that we should follow our intuition.

If something feels right for you, then open 'the door' and embrace that path, if you don't you might miss something you have to learn, or to meet someone. This learning can be good or bad, but it is a learning just the same. Things can go wrong, things can go right: do not fret over things you cannot control. This municipal Albergue was very clean and comfortable.

The next morning, I left after breakfast for Villa de Mazariffe, which is an alternative route, variant, where I would meet again the Camino Skies' group. It was cold but sunny. At one stage, I missed a turn and ended up in another village. There were many birds along the way keeping me company, before I realised I was on the wrong path and I walked back, and followed a long flat, gravelly path. One will never know!

On both sides there were fields of colza with their yellow flowers in bloom. The red poppies were everywhere, spring was definitely back. My heart was singing. The mountains were still covered with snow. I arrived at an intersection with a yellow arrow painted on the road, and I took it. It was a trick, as this arrow did not lead me to the path but to a busy café. So: beware, the cunningness of the human being!

There was a sense of heaviness in this café; it was the first time that I felt such heaviness in a coffee place since the beginning of my pilgrimage.

The pilgrims were in groups and did not try to connect with others. I sat for a while, and drank my coffee, before starting again, then traced back my steps to the intersection and reached the Villa de Mazariffe without any problems.

I had the name of an Albergue and stopped there waiting for the group. I met Bernadette who lives just outside Geneva, Switzerland, Helen from Germany and many others. The Albergue was packed. Bernadette had her hands on her heart and bought a meal for Juan, a Mexican pilgrim, as he had no money.

I was waiting for the group; the hours passed and there was no sign of them. I was getting worried when Cheryl appeared. There had been a change, they had tried to contact me by phone but my French sim card did not work, again. Cheryl was super excited and at the same time anxious as she was waiting for a phone call, about a work position for when she returned home. Her phone rang, she left us and returned all jubilant. She got the position she was hoping for. We all cheered and congratulated her. I was so happy for her. I returned to my lodging, and met the group the next morning for breakfast.

I walked with the crew. Some sections of the trail were straight, built on asphalt, with fields on both sides, and stony trails. We stopped for coffee after the famous and impressive Roman Bridge, Paso Honroso with its 19 arches before Hospital del Orbigo: a town so clean and peaceful with lovely parks. After a little incline, we reached Santibanez de Valdeiglesias where I stopped eight years ago, but we did not stay in the same Albergue. At that time there was only one Albergue, nowadays there are two.

The crew informed me that they would interview me later in the afternoon in a field just behind the Albergue. They were concerned about the light. Answering their questions, some moments of my married life came into my mind like an impetuous current. After an unfortunate and untimely incident my life changed forever and a part of the 'Little Claude' died.

Thirty-four years later, my marriage broke down and at the age of 58, I became a check out chick which led me to know about the Camino. It took me many years to resolve and heal this part of my life. Thanks to my first Camino, I was able to re-discover the

'Little Claude' as a strong, independent human being. I was shaken. Before the interview, I had thought that I had resolved everything during my first Camino. We finished the interview and I informed the crew that I needed to be totally by myself the next day. I was shocked to realise that there were still some parts of my heart that had not healed when I thought they had.

I left alone, as agreed the night before for Saint Catalina da Somoza. The crew had respected my wishes and I was thankful to them. Leaving the near flat path behind me, I was back into high altitudes with their uphills and downhills, forests, ploughed fields and some green wheat fields too. I was hoping to see 'Davide'. I had met him so many years ago, at that time he was known on the path, for his generosity and care for the pilgrims. He was living in a derelict barn and out the front there was a stand with organic foods, drinks, cereals, nuts and fruit, as well as some hot water for coffee and tea with a 'Donativo Box' so that you could give what you could afford. From Santibanez de Valdeiglesias to Astorga there are about 15 kilometres. The only coffee shop in the village was closed and I was dying for a coffee when I arrived at this spot; it was like an angel was looking after the weary pilgrims. This time, I could not recognise the place. The barn had been repaired; there were young people everywhere, there were many stands. It had become a very busy place. I did meet 'Davide' again. Though still welcoming, I saw some changes. I was half surprised as he had become a celebrity appearing in movies and other well publicised events. Somehow, I missed the old 'Davide'.

At the top of a plateau, we could see Astorga with the surrounding mountains. At this intersection, a not so young man, with a typical Spanish hat on his head, was playing some Spanish songs to the delight of the passing pilgrims. It was midday when I arrived at Astorga which is the cross-roads for the Camino of the Via de la Plata from Seville in Andalusia and the Camino Frances. Cheryl, Julie, Phoebe, Fergus and Noel were having a coffee on the main square and I joined them. After lunch, we separated as Julie and Cheryl were being filmed. Passing in front of the Romanesque Cathedral of Santa Maria, I heard some music and decided to go inside. There was a mass taking place, and it was packed with parishioners. Next to the Cathedral stands the neo-medieval Episcopal

Palace, designed by the famous Gaudi, considered as the architect of God.

I was on my way to Santa-Catalina-de-Somoza, when along a long stretch of road, I crossed paths with Alexander. We walked together; we were staying at the same Albergue. Cheryl, Alexander, other pilgrims and I were staying in the same room. There was a lovely internal garden in the middle of the Albergue. I took the decision to change the dressing on my feet and toes in this peaceful environment. After this little daily ritual, I went to the lounge room where I saw Alexander drawing on a tablet. His drawing was quite similar to the one I had received on my mobile so many weeks ago. The penny dropped. Alexander was the person who had sent me the drawing, with the words: 'A butterfly Camino Angel on the Camino', after we had met in Pamplona. Since that day, I had always wondered who had sent me this drawing, as I had crossed paths with quite a few 'Alexanders'. Here was the one. I was baffled, and excited, and I thanked him for sending me his first drawing, with such an amazing meaning. He showed me the other ones he had done during his Camino. I was in total awe of his skill. Previously, his art had been exhibited in galleries and he was planning to show the ones he had drawn about his Camino on his return to The Netherlands. I, then, returned to the dormitory and started to check my backpack and have it ready for the next day. I was checking all my items when I realised that one plastic bag was missing. It was the one which contained all the things I needed to care for my feet. I had hurt the tendons in my ankle weeks before leaving Australia and had treatment done to help heal them. I had bought many A.N.F. therapy discs as they needed to be replaced every few days. They were helping me to control the pain and as well they had been pretty expensive.

I put all that was in my backpack on my bunk, emptying every section, checking and rechecking every pocket. I could not find them. I became frantic. I needed them to be able to finish my Camino. I went back to the area where I had cared for my toes and feet but they were not there. I asked everyone in the adjacent dormitories as well as the members of our group, but no one had seen this little plastic bag. I contacted the owners of the Albergue, just in case, without success. I was desperate. Seeing my desperation, two young girls asked their pilgrims' group. No one had seen the little bag. I went back to my room, checked again and laid on my bunk, worrying, I fell asleep.

The next morning, I put my backpack at the entrance to the dining room and went to have my breakfast. I was undoing the zip of the top compartment of my backpack to put in my lunch, when I saw the little plastic bag with the therapy discs, and the bandages all intact. I could not believe it. I had checked all sections of my backpack, so many times, the previous night even some pilgrims had seen me doing the checking and it was not there. Had someone heard that I had lost it, found it then put it back in my backpack? Why was it not given back to me personally instead of putting it back in my backpack? Who? I quickly stopped myself from thinking these unkind thoughts. I did not want to think about this episode anymore and soil my soul and I left the Albergue.

Outside, it was still dark and I started walking, in the direction of El Acebo. I crossed El Ganso with its old, derelict houses. I met a young French man, Maurice. He was walking the Camino for spiritual reasons. Our conversations ended up about spirituality and how the world that has lost its direction with the big corporations and industries, wanting more profit year after year, without any thought for their workers or employees. Their wants are their only driving force. It cannot keep on going this way, or poverty will be the result in many nations. Equilibrium needs to be restored before it is too late. From the past history of the world we know what anger can create.

We arrived at Foncebadon. The village was buzzing with so many pilgrims coming from everywhere. There were many new cafes along the main street. If the derelict houses were not there, I would not have recognised the place. I stopped at a cafe for a little while and kept on walking towards the famous Cruzo de Ferro which is one of the most symbolic sites and the highest point of the Camino Frances at 1,517 metres.

At the top of an enormous cairn there is a cross. Pilgrims from all around the world place a little stone from their home or a personal object, a symbol of freeing themselves of personal burdens and starting anew. It is a tradition dating to before the Roman conquest, and which continued with the Christian pilgrims in the Middle Ages.

Months earlier, I was walking in Mount-Cootha, near Brisbane, Australia, with some friends, when I saw a heart-shaped stone and picked it up. I had kept it and, I decided to carry it and deposit it at this very special place on the Way, for my little family and for all the people I love, who love me, or who had loved me. For me, this little heart-shaped stone represented forgiveness for all those who had hurt me during my lifetime and if anyone might hurt me in the future, as I will forgive them too.

I wanted this little stone to heal them. People hurt you if they are unhappy with their life and have not found solace in their soul. I wish that one day they will find peace and become more loving to the people crossing their path. At the base of the cross, I prayed and imagined a 'Dove' symbol of peace taking away my sadness and the sadness of others. It could be so easy and at the same time difficult to love each other. I prayed for peace in the world. You could say: 'Wishful thinking!' One can only hope.

At Cruzo de Ferro, I met Julie, Susan and part of the crew. We chatted for a while then I started descending towards El Acebo following a stony trail and some wooded areas. The panorama from there is majestic. Seeing these mountains again, which look so much like those of my birth place, lifted my heart once more.

At the bottom of a hill, there was a little stand and a 'donativo' box and beside it a wooden bench for the pilgrims to rest. There was no one looking after the little stand - it was based on trust and honesty. There were many rosaries, statuettes, prayer cards, Buddhist prayer flags, water bottles and in a small basket some bananas. I took a wooden rosary and left a donation in the little box.

The road to El Acebo followed a dirt and rocky path; I could see some pilgrims walking there. We waved at each other and met again at Monjardin. Arlette had hurt herself along the Way. Her face was full of scratches and she had difficulty walking. She wanted to finish the walk with her husband and so they decided to take the road for more security. It would not have been so pleasant walking on the road, but it was better to be safe than sorry.

I entered the refuge of Monjardin. Thomas, a Knight Templar, looks after the refuge with the help of some volunteers. I had met him in 2010 in the courtyard but this time I went in, I had a coffee and as in the Medieval Tradition, on 'Donativo basis'. I looked around; they were selling many small items.

I met a Canadian pilgrim and we noticed that cleanliness was not their first priority.

After ascending the steep hill I saw El Acebo village with its slate roofs. I did not recognise the entrance of the village. I had to cross the village to find the lodging which was at the other end. It was a new and very modern refuge. I was relieved to know that we were not staying at the same place where I had stopped eight years ago. What happened at that Albergue? It was about 4.00am when we were woken up by very loud music coming from outside the refuge. A pilgrim went out and found the culprit. The music was coming from a locked car. We could not do anything about it and everyone left in the night.

I was looking forward to the next day's walk. I left with Greg and Julie. I knew it was a difficult section, downhill to Molinesca with a difference of 1.000 m altitude, going through quaint villages, beautiful forests and a steep section of challenging sharp and pointy stones where you could very easily get hurt. You can avoid it by taking the road. I wanted to stop again at 'Mahou' a lovely peaceful coffee place. Sadly, it was not meant to be, as the path had been re-directed so the pilgrims would not go through the steepest and hardest section I had to climb down to reach Molinesca. Spring was there in all its glory, with flowers in the fields, growing along the path between the stone walls showing us resilience and strength: through somewhat difficult times, we can survive no matter what.

The quaint little villages have not changed along that section. To my amazement, I arrived in front of the Church, and in no time crossed the Bridge over the Rio Meruelo and met Gilbert from Austria. He had broken off with his girlfriend and decided to take the Camino to try to heal his heart. His lovely family encouraged him to do so. He will take over the family business on his return if he sees fit, though he was not pushed to do so. He was a very gentle soul and I hoped that before he finished his Camino he would find peace and know which direction to take for his future. The Camino brings healing to many. It is such a safe way to leave your burdens on the side of the road bit by bit and return anew! We do not forget, but we can find peace in our heart and walk the rest of our life with a lighter step.

Arriving at Ponferrada, capital of the Bierzo Region, I could not find the lodging and wandered for quite a while in this city before finding my way. With the problems, I had with my phone, I could not contact anyone, but once again I was helped, as I bumped into a pilgrim who was staying in the same Albergue as the group. After my chores, I went to visit the impressive castle built by the Knights Templar and founded by monks during the 12th and 13th century as the group went visiting the city to buy some food.

I walked with the crew the next day. We did not take the scenic route and walked mostly along the road. At the entrance to Villafranca del Bierzo, in the provinces of Castile and Leon, there is the 12th and 13th century Romanesque church of Santiago of the Apostles. If the Church is open you can go under the famous 'Puerta del Pedron' (Door of forgiveness) so all your sins will be forgiven. No chance this time as the church was closed. Later on, we met Cheryl who could not find the path. Villafranca del Bierzo is known as the 'Little Santiago de Compostela'. It is a beautiful town. As usual, after our dinner, I attended to my poor feet and went to bed, ready for the next day.

The next morning, Ray and I left together. His dream was to buy a house in Spain. He was tired, slower at times, and at other times it was me. We walked for quite a while together, till we separated; the pilgrims are protected from the speedy cars by concrete barriers along a stream. Your feet would love to paddle in it if you decide to descend the embankment. There are many derelict houses which added a 'je ne sais quoi' to the walk and you almost forget the pain under your feet as you are walking mostly along bitumen roads. Some have beautiful geranium pots on their window-ledges reminding me of my place of birth. I arrived at Las Herrias, as usual, the last one. The other members had settled in their normal routine and were at the terrace of a café having a drink. At the Albergue, I met a young lovely French girl, who was a volunteer. The Camino Frances has become so popular. Spanish people and others from around the world had seen an opportunity and bought old farms, and refurbished them for the pilgrims - so private refuges had sprung up along the Way. Consequently, many have difficulty surviving.

The next day was going to be an arduous stretch; we would reach O'Ceibrero then keep on going to Fonfria. I was starting to feel very, very tired. I had lost two toe-nails, and looking at my feet, I could see I would lose more before I reached Santiago. I left the

Albergue early and walked for a little while with a lady from Belgium, Monique. In front of me, Noel, with his precious friend 'the camera' was showing me resilience, as carrying it most of the time was a challenge in itself. Ray was walking with him. Soon they disappeared. I made sure this time that I would not miss the little dirt path as I did the first time to reach O'Ceibrero. I did not fancy climbing up to the bitumen road again. It is a very small dirt mountain trail that you find on your left-hand side after the village of Laguna De Castilla and it can be very easily missed.

The climb and its path up to O'Ceibrero are at times challenging, but in the same way so beautiful with its stunning landscape of mountains, similar to the Pyrenees. It was spring and the mountains were in bloom creating a painting of purple colours as far as your eyes could see. It was absolutely gorgeous. I huffed and puffed. I stopped a lot enjoying the scenery, before starting again, wondering when the climb along this rocky path would ever end. As we know, one step at a time, we reached the top. As I arrived at the entrance of O'Ceibrero I saw a landmark indicating that you are in Galicia and have left the Castile region. I entered the village with its thatched roofs and round 'Pallozas' (houses), when I met an American couple. They were walking the Camino with their two grand-sons aged 10 and 11 years old. What beautiful memories and lessons they were giving to these boys! We had met before. To my amazement, these young ones were never tired and always managed to play at the end of their day's walk. The family was very excited as they were waiting for the boys 'mother and father as well their baby brother only a few months old. The whole family would walk the rest of the Camino to reach Santiago together. The boys showed me how they had planned to pull their baby brother's pram by putting a thick rope around their waist. I wished them 'Buen Camino'. Amazing!

I stopped at a café and met Noel, Ray and Julie. No time to visit much, as after a little respite and a bit of lunch the four of us walked towards Fonfria. I knew that the first 10 kilometres after O'Ceibrero were like a handsaw with its ups and downs, and at times stony difficult trails. We passed stone Celtic houses and villages. After the Hospital da Condesa, we arrived at Alto de San Roque at an elevation of 1,270 metres with the famous statue of a pilgrim fending off the winds and took the traditional photo. After a steep hill we reached Alto do Poio, the highest point of Galicia at 1,337 metres. From there, it was all downhill. It was cold and rainy when we arrived at Fonfria. I was so tired that I could not utter one single word. As soon as I arrived, I laid on my bunk for a while before my body recuperated and regained the energy and strength to go for a shower. I had walked no more than 21 km, but it was a hard section. The Albergue, at Fonfria, is absolutely gorgeous and an experience in itself.

The next day, Noel and I left together; it was very cold and overcast. Outside the Albergue, a farmer was taking his herd of cattle out of their stable. Seeing us the cows went left and right, scaring the other pilgrims. I approached one of them and patted it: a reminder of my past, when a few flakes of snow started to fall. Noel had never felt snowflakes on his face. It was so beautiful to see his joy and amazement: a magical moment on the Camino.

From Fonfria, it is constantly downhill. At the end of the village, I did not see, the elderly lady who used to put some pancakes in your hands. You would have thought it was a gift, but not at all, as she would forcefully ask for some money. You had no time to react. She was quite an expert. She was not there.

She could have been still in bed - it was, probably too early or too cold. We climbed down for a long while till Filloval, enjoying the beautiful views of the valley and its surrounding mountains, through forests and shady paths. We passed through many villages on dirt roads till we reached Tricastela.

Julie and Greg had decided to take the variant route through Samos. We took San Xil. The landscape is scenic all the way, going through little hamlets with their greyish slates roofs, the fields were so green. We passed more little villages, crossing streams over bridges, climbing steep inclines and downhill, bends and turns. Magical scenery all the way and we arrived at Sarria. Santiago was not too far now, only 115 km.

Sarria is a very busy place. Many pilgrims start from there, for various reasons, such as work or family commitments. Once they reach Santiago de Compostela they can request their certificate called 'Compostela' which proves that they have walked the Camino de Santiago. If you start from Sarria, you need two stamps per day on your pilgrim's passport. The many cafes along that section have stamp and pad at your disposal on their counter so you can put a stamp on your document. After walking so many days in nature and its quietness, I always have difficulty readjusting to the city busyness and its noise.

Sarria to Portamarin: still so cold, some rain, beautiful green landscape. When you live in Australia, the driest continent on earth, the colour green is stupendous and you appreciate it much more; your eyes seem to pick up all the different shades of green. I walked with Julie, as well as with June and Dean, two delightful family members of one of the group who were going to walk the last 100 - 115 kilometres. I enjoyed not only meeting them but the conversation I had with June, Dean was more reserved. This section is very beautiful passing more small hamlets and typical Celtic villages, with its fences made of stones. Some houses look like derelict to us, though people still live there. You see many well-behaved cows sharing your path, walking quietly one behind the other with the 'head' in the front with a big bell hanging on its collar. You also see some little 'horreos' typical of Galicia. What is a 'horreo'? It is a Galician granary built in wood or stone and raised from the ground up by stumps and flat stones to keep rodents out. You will find some small or very large ones all over Galicia.

We stopped at a little restaurant for lunch before separating. The flow of pilgrims was growing, even though it was only mid-May. At one stage, I checked a little shop and saw an Australian flag. I bought it. Was it a little 'clin d'oeil' (a wink) from Australia? I was walking with my little family, back in Australia, in my heart, hoping that one day one or more of them will walk the Camino. After the downhill climb, and crossing the famous Portomarin Bridge, there are two ways to reach the town. I had climbed the stairs leading to the town before and so I decided to take the other way. It did not happen as I could not find it and walked the stairs again and went to the lodging and re-joined the group. The next day, we would reach Palas del Rei. We were getting so close to Santiago, it was hard to believe. Even given how painful my body was, I did not want to see the end of my pilgrimage. I had the same feeling of sadness as in 2010.

Every morning, I spent a lot of time attending to my feet, so I left even later than usual, after the others. I crossed the Rio Mino over a long, metal foot bridge and followed the path through the forest, mostly on dirt and rocks, uphill and downhill. At times, I walked along a stream where little birds shared the path, and gave me a free concert. The flow of pilgrims was getting bigger and bigger.

An advantage being part of a group, and staying in private lodgings was that I did not have to be worried about the 'bunk hunt' which allowed me to take my time. All the pilgrims were wearing rain gear; it was so cold and misty. I crossed paths with a young man from Liverpool, then with Lin, a young Vietnamese lady living in America. For Lin, she wanted to walk the Camino, before her wedding in a few weeks' time.

I received a message from my son, David amazingly my phone was working again! My mother's heart was flying high.

The highest point of this stretch is at Sierra de Ligonde where you find the supposedly most famous cross on the Camino Frances dating from the 17th century. There are hundreds of reasons why someone would want to walk the Camino de Santiago. Each one of us walks for our own personal reasons.

Some do not know what their reason is and they find out later, for some it is a calling, for others it is to find which role they have to play in this world. If they have been through a difficult time in their life, they want to sort themselves out. Maybe they went through a challenging illness, or the loss of a loved one. I arrived at Palas del Rei mid-afternoon.

In the dormitory, there were more pilgrims and more snoring. Consequently, in the morning you do not leave rested. This is the part of the Camino where you learn to be more humble towards others. Some pilgrims are quite annoyed by this lullaby, and can be quite rude towards that person, not knowing that they are snoring themselves.

More uphill and downhills, paved and bitumen tracks, streams, beautiful trees and fields covered with spring flowers gorgeous, idyllic villages. Before Leboreiro, you leave the region of Lugo and enter the province of A Coruna. Next to the small medieval Church of Santa Maria you see the replica of the first 'horreos', used many thousands of years ago. It is shaped like a wicker-basket with a thatched cover. At La Huella, there was a stand with memorabilia. The attendant put a seal on my Pilgrims' passport with two hearts intertwined and a tiny piece of ribbon and a little heart with an arrow running through it. To me it represented the life of any human being. Who has not had their heart broken during their life and maybe later has found solace with another person? I had walked with Renee, Justin and Marie for most of the day. They were very funny and our laughter would have resonated in the entire forest at the joy of the birds as they joined us with their songs.

Many pilgrims stopped at Melide to enjoy their speciality 'Pulpo' which is a boiled octopus. At every corner, every café, it is sold as a delicacy. Needless to say that I ran away from this town, as I am anaphylactic with all sea-food and on the top of that I had to go through its dreaded modern suburbia. The town 'Melide' is at the junction of two Caminos: the Primitivo, an inside route that starts and finishes in Spain, and the Frances. The Camino Primitivo is the shortest of all the Caminos in Spain. After Melide, I crossed the eucalyptus forests with their intense aroma which reminded me of Australia and the approaching ending of my journey with the group. After more ascents and descents, I arrived at Ribadiso.

After a somewhat restless night, as my body, my legs and my feet were hurting so much, we left Ribadiso. Nothing was going to defeat me. Noel and I left the lodging under a blue sky on a very cold day. With determination, one may say, stubbornness, I started walking with my trekking posts at a sturdy pace.

Somewhere along the way, in the middle of a forest, we saw a little paradise with armchairs, tables, and a van selling coffee. We took this opportunity to have a bit of respite, have a coffee and we met Spiritual from Romania with his wife, Marianne. They were doing their Camino on bicycle; we had a deep and profound talk about gratitude, in this little corner of paradise which warmed my heart. Soon Noel and I arrived at O'Perdrouzo. The end of our pilgrimage and documentary was round the corner. All would be over the next day.

On the last day, we left together, but soon I found myself alone. I tried to catch up with them by walking faster, but they were too fast. Come on, Claude, a bit more effort, when an awful pain crossed the lower part of my leg. I had developed some pain in that area some days earlier, but did not take care of it. However, today, the pain had worsened; maybe walking faster had created more injury. I had developed Shin Splints. This was not going to stop me. I crossed many hamlets and eucalyptus forests, there were more climbs, asphalt roads and gravel tracks. I arrived at Monto do Gozo 'Hill of Joy' and its busyness. In 1989, Pope John Paul II had united 500,000 young people for

World Youth Day. After the traditional photo, I left Monto do Gozo for Santiago de Compostela. It was going to be the last time I walked with the group. My feelings were the same as I had in 2010. I did not want to see the end of my pilgrimage.

It was 17 May 2018. I still had many days before returning to France and staying with my sister who was on holidays at the time. I had planned to keep on walking after Santiago. I had plenty of time left in front of me and had thought about it, but had put this idea on hold. Once, I reached Santiago de Compostela, my decision was made: I will keep on walking, my heart felt lighter, though the pain in my leg was a reminder of my injury. Just like before, I would not listen. One never learns!

As I was entering Santiago, alone, there was some festivity with music and dancers, in their Celtic costumes. I admired and enjoyed their dances, then kept on walking towards the Cathedral.

The crew welcomed me with their camera, as well as many pilgrims who I had met along the Way. We hugged, laughed, with tears rolling down our cheeks. The emotion of reaching Santiago was as powerful as the first time. My mind flew back to the challenges, the pain, and the beautiful meetings I had experienced. Every bit was worth it.

We left the square and re-joined some members of the group, with June and Dean, at the terrace of a café, and went to our lodging. Later on, Fergus asked me if I would mind interviewing a French pilgrim, Patrick, who was staying at the same Albergue as us. With great pleasure, I accepted being able to help. At the end of the interview, the crew told me that I missed my profession, as I was so talented! I loved it, even at 72 years old; you do not know your abilities. Well, if there are many lives, I might return as an interviewer or journalist!

I went back to the dormitory, across from my bunk was a lovely lady Leonne from Canada. I could sense her sadness and approached her. It was not a coincidence that we met. As there was no one in the dormitory, we were able to have a heart to heart conversation. Leonne had decided to walk her Camino after reading 'Hidden Treasures' from a Canadian writer, Louise Dupont. Louise had written her book after her son's suicide, André, aged 21. Leonne was very sad to see the end of her journey and to return to our world among other things. She has found again: 'La joie de

Vivre' thanks to the Camino and we sang. Leonne has learnt a lot about herself and her strength. Her life was going to be different from now on. Leonne became, and has remained, a member of my Camino family. I have been blessed to have met her, our friendship will last forever. After my return to Australia, I was invited as a guest-speaker to a group and there I met an Australian lady who is her friend: serendipity! Life, with its mysterious ways, always amazes me.

As a group, we had our last meal together, at a restaurant in the centre of Santiago. The following morning, Susan was returning to Australia and I went to buy a birthday cake. Julie and I had our birthday in April, and so I decided to celebrate our April birthdays at the end of our Camino and in the same time our return to our respective countries. This was perfect. A great way to finish our pilgrimage!

The next morning, I was up at the crack of dawn to say good-bye to Susan as I did not know if I would ever see her again. Eventually, we did at the Camino Skies' preview, in February 2019, in Melbourne, Australia.

That same morning, I went with Noel and Fergus to the Cathedral where an English mass was going to be celebrated in one of the little side-chapels. We were asked to introduce ourselves, and why we had done the pilgrimage. The priest approached me, and said:

"Claude, it would mean a lot if you could read a prayer for us"

What a blessing! The magic of the Camino was continuing.

After the mass, Fergus, Noel and I went to collect my Compostela, which I should have received the previous day. One day difference on my Compostela did not mean much to me.

The group, with the exception of Susan, rented a van and travelled to Finisterre. When we arrived at our private lodging, I was surprised to see that I had taken the photo of this place when I passed in front of it in 2010.

I was sharing a bedroom with Cheryl. As I entered the bedroom, on my bed, there was a little packet, I opened it and saw a little metal plaque with the following inscription:

'Camino de Santiago CLAUDE'

It was a present from Cheryl. Just imagine my surprise, a plaque with my name inscribed on it. Cheryl told me that she was walking in Santiago when she looked in a shop window and noticed the plaque with my name on it. Immediately, she thought of me and bought it. I was so touched by such a kind and beautiful gesture. It was incredible. I asked her if she had it stamped. 'No, it was just there with your name on it' was her answer.

The Camino is incredible with its magical moments. To have found this plaque with my name on it was unbelievable. In Spanish it should have been stamped 'Claudia' or for a male: 'Claudio'. The Camino will take your heart away in various ways. Needless to say, I was so touched by such kindness. I thanked her and hugged her, feeling so amazingly blessed. Late after dinner, Noel, Phoebe, Julie and I went to the beach to take some shots of the area.

The next morning, I was up at 4.00am to say good bye to Fergus, June, Dean and Cheryl who were returning to Santiago to fly back to Australia or New Zealand. After breakfast, I took my backpack, hugged and said: 'Good bye' to the rest of the group and walked towards Lires. As Phoebe was still asleep, I asked Noel to give her my best wishes for a bright future. Phoebe had been an important part of our group.

Camino Skies' Group

I have to say as I was leaving them, I felt a little tug in my heart. They had been part of my life for a while and I wished them all, the best for the rest of their personal life. However, from then on, I would be able to walk at my own pace and with a free mind, as I was always arriving later than the others and this had been a constant worry for me.

The Itinerary: 34 Days
The Camino Frances
Saint-Jean-Pied-De-Port – Santiago de Compostela with Camino Skies

The number of kilometres walked varies from guide-book to guide-book. For this reason, I will not add them

Day	From	To
1	Saint Jean-Pied-de-Port	Orisson
2	Valcarlos	Roncesvalles
3	Roncesvalles	Zubiri
4	Zubiri	Pamplona
5	Pamplona	Estella

Day	From	To
6	Estella	Los Arcos
7	Los Arcos	Viana
8	Viana	Navarette
9	Navarrete	Azofra
10	Azofra	Granon
11	Granon	Villiambistia
12	Villiambistia	Ages
13	Ages	Burgos
14	Burgos	Hornillos del Camino
15	Hornillos del Camino	Fromista
16	Fromista	Carrion des Condes

Day	From	To
17	Carrion des Condes	Ledigos
18	Ledigos	Berciamo del Camino
19	Berciamo del Camino	Reliegos
20	Reliegos	Leon
21	Leon	Virgen del Camino
22	Virgen del Camino	Villar Mazarife (Variante)
23	Mazarife	Santibanez Valdeiglesias
24	Santibanez Valdeiglesias	Santa Catalina de Sonoza
25	Santa Catalina de Sonoza	El Acebo
26	El Acebo	Ponferrada
27	Ponferrada	Villafranca del Berzio

Day	From	To
28	Villafranca del Berzio	Las Herrias
29	Las Herrias	Fonfria
30	Fonfria	Sarria
31	Sarria	Portomarin
32	Portomarin	Palas del Rei
33	Palas del Rei	Ribadiso da Baixo
34	Ribadiso da Baixo	Santiago de Compostela
35	Santiago de Compostela	Finisterre (by car)

CHAPTER 4

Walking alone in Spain

Finisterre – Muxia – Dumbria – Santiago de Compostela

10 days: 18 May 2018 - 28 May 2018
at 72 years of age

Walking along that path, I felt that my love for Galicia was still the same. It is very similar to where I was born in France, and my heart started to sing again. I met three pilgrims. The shin splint in my leg was getting worse and I had to walk slower. I would stop at Lires. I was crossing a forest with a lot of dead branches lying on the ground. I picked a sturdy branch to replace one of my missing trekking poles. Someone at the Albergue, in Santiago, had broken one of my poles. Whoever did this never left a note of apology.

After walking quite a while, I saw a shelter for buses with a bench and stopped for some respite. I was eating a piece of fruit, when out of nowhere appeared

Xavier, from Germany. We had stayed in the same Albergue in Virgen del Camino. He was coming from Muxia to finish his Camino at Finisterre. Xavier noticed my wooden stick. As soon as I mentioned what had happened, he pulled his two trekking poles out of his backpack and handed them over to me.

Surprised, I refused. Xavier insisted that I take them. He was returning to Germany the following day. I tried to convince him to take the one I had, but he vehemently refused. From there, I carried three poles. I was quite safe if anything happened to any of the trekking poles. I would always have a spare one. I thanked and hugged him as we went our own way. My steps took me through beautiful forest lanes, downhills and uphills, farmlands, and small hamlets with their famous 'horreos': graneries.

I had not booked accommodation at Lires and returned to where I had stopped in 2010. Unfortunately, it was full. My only choice was an Albergue a little bit further on, after a steep hill. There, I met Gillian, 80 years old. Gillian had written a book about her divorce and her life. She believed in angels, and many lives.

Her guide was 'Sai Baba'. As she was sharing her story, I felt a jolt in my heart, with the similarities of her life and mine.

At breakfast, the following morning, I shared with Gillian that, along the path, I had met a lady called 'Lisa' from America. While walking alone, one day, I was thinking about her story, and saw a heart-shaped stone and picked it up for her. I had hoped to meet her again; sadly, up to that point it never happened and probably will not happen now. Gillian replied: 'One never knows, Claude!'

We hugged and I left for Muxia. A male pilgrim, seeing me leaving the Albergue with my backpack, told me my bag was too heavy and as usual, I smiled.

A few kilometres, after Lires, under a porch, there was a stand, with a sign: 'Have a coffee, on the house'. I thought it was too soon after Lires and I passed by. Later on, I regretted my decision so much as there was nothing for many kilometres, and the more I walked, the more I was dying for a coffee.

Along the way, I met Liu, a young Korean woman; we had crossed paths a few times. It was the end of her Camino. Her emotions were too great and she cried on my shoulder. I could understand her feeling to the fullest.

I was getting closer to Muxia when I saw a couple at a little table and on it was a display of fruit and a jug of coffee. I put my backpack down and started chatting with two young Canadian pilgrims. I had my back turned and did not see a lady coming from the opposite direction when I heard: 'Claude, Claude my Camino Angel'

I jumped and turned. It was 'Lisa', who was walking from Muxia to Finisterre. She had travelled by bus to Muxia that same morning. I could not believe it. I was so happy to see her again and gave her the little heart-shaped stone that I had collected for her.

Talk about coincidence, can you believe it? 'Lisa' had decided to walk from Muxia to Finisterre that same morning and had taken the bus from Santiago to Muxia. Had she walked from Finisterre to Muxia, our paths would have never crossed again as we would have been walking in the same direction! That same morning, I had put my wish and desire in the Universe or God to meet 'Lisa' again. Sometimes things fall into place as if by magic.

The pain in my leg had worsened and I looked for a lodging not too far from the Cape of Muxia, as this would allow me to be closer so I could walk up to the Church of Nosa Senora da Barca along the seaside promenade and climb Mount Corpino.

It was at the top of Mount Corpino eight years ago, that I had released all my emotional pain and found peace, forgiving all the persons who had hurt me during my life, as without forgiveness I would not have been able to walk freely along my new path. There, I left a heart-shaped stone, close to a boulder and a thistle, about 10 centimetres tall and I wanted to see if I could find it again.

My feet led me to the Albergue of Bela Muxia. I took possession of my bunk. I left right away for the Cape of Muxia. The church was closed and I climbed Mount Corpino where, at the top, the energy and the peace you feel are tremendous. I noticed a young man, Ernst from Germany, and I asked him to take my photo and we conversed on a spiritual level, opportunities and coincidences in life, sitting on a stone, admiring the 360 degree views above Muxia and its harbour. Ernst left and I started to look for the boulder and thistle where I deposited my little heart-shaped-stone so many years ago. The 10 centimetre thistle had grown into an enormous bush. With a little stick I scratched under the bush, hoping to find my little heart, with no luck. I had deposited it there in the hope that it would be protected from the wind as I wanted to protect my heart during the rest of my life. I may say it has been well shielded.

I looked for another shady spot and placed another heart-shaped-stone before ascending Mount Corpino. Sitting on a huge boulder, beside the church, I looked at the raging ocean; it was battering the shore with its tempestuous and fierce waves, like a furious demon. But I knew that if I looked below on the floor of the ocean all would be calm and peaceful. Just the opposite of what I was so many years ago. From the outside I looked so peaceful, though so sad and disenchanted about life. Seated close to the shore, I revisited my life from far back with its chaos, obstacles and the tough challenges I faced. The small steps and small goals I had achieved and all the changes that had happened after my first Camino were evident. Looking at the magnificent sunset, I could see the big picture right in front of me as if I had stepped into a different level of consciousness. I let the waves take my past and dragged it far away forever, so it would not hurt anymore. I sat there for a while, waiting for the moon to appear and slowly, following the ocean, I walked back to my lodging.

With my leg more swollen and painful I did not sleep too well. The next morning, I met Samantha from Liverpool. I did not have any food and she shared her breakfast with me, as she was returning to England that day and gave me the rest of her packed food.

Later on, Alexandra from Brazil approached me. She was doing her Camino with her boyfriend on bicycles. She shared with me their challenges as they followed the path and were not cycling along the roads. I had the idea that doing the Camino on bicycle was so much easier. My conversation with Alexandra changed my view.

On my first Camino, after walking 100 days, my body had said: 'No more' and I had to listen to it and finished my pilgrimage at Muxia. This time, I decided that I would walk back to Santiago no matter what. I was eight years older, but still as determined as before. The owner of the Albergue, saw me limping, with my swollen leg and told me to stop walking. I replied: 'I want to walk back to Santiago. I was not able to do it the first time, but this time no matter what, I will do it. I will go through Dumbria as I have walked twice along the Muxia Way'. He replied: 'With a leg like yours, it is madness'. He suggested that I go with a couple by taxi to the next little village or near to the next village, which would reduce the distance to walk by a few kilometres that day as they were returning to Santiago. Miracle: I agreed!

If you walk from Finisterre to Muxia, you can see the arrows indicating each direction very clearly. I was expecting the same on the Dumbria path, if you want to walk back to Santiago de Compostela. To my surprise the path was signed only for the pilgrims walking from Santiago to Muxia. I did not have a GPS or a guide book, just a small map, which was showing only a line that I found in the Albergue. I had to trust, like at the beginning of my first pilgrimage across France, that all would be well. I crossed paths with three pilgrims coming from Santiago. The countryside was beautiful, I got lost many times. Somehow I did not care very much, up to when I crossed a forest and could not find my way out of it at all. I psyched myself up, to take away the fear of my body, turned left, right, left, and so on for quite a while. There was no one around. I was hoping to hear some cars, so I could walk in the direction of the noise of the traffic. No chance! After walking for two hours or so in that forest, I started to be more than agitated when I saw a very little dirt path and decided to take it. When you are lost, you lose your sense of distance; your best bet is to keep on walking and hope for the best and pray.

Suddenly, I started to hear the noise of trucks and cars. Courage Claude, you are saved! I went in the direction of the noisy cars and arrived at an intersection. I was hoping to find some signage for the direction to Dumbria. Wishful thinking, so I decided to turn right as there was a little path following the highway. After walking about one hour or more, I saw across the highway a man working in his garden. Carefully I crossed the highway and asked my way.

The Spanish man scratched his head and in sign language told me that I should take the opposite direction. I thanked him, not without asking him, which city I would have reached if I had kept walking in the direction I was on. He answered: 'Lires'. I thought: Trust you, Claude, you still have a very good sense of direction and chuckled at myself.

I crossed the highway and started walking back till I reached the intersection when I got out of the forest. Now my dilemma started again. I had two options: either return back across the forest or walk along the highway where you could see huge signposts showing 'forbidden to walkers and pilgrims'.

This time it was me who was scratching my head. The embankment was not wider than my backpack without any protection. I did not wish to go back to the forest so I started walking along the highway. I would not advise anyone to do this as it is pretty dangerous.

Clearly, I had no choice. The cars and trucks were travelling at 130 km per hour. We have to walk in the opposite direction from the traffic and soon I realised I could finish under the wheels of the trucks as they were lifting me up when passing me by. In case this happened, I did not want to remember which vehicle would lift me or if I would end up under their wheels, so I pulled my cap in front of my eyes, as far as I could. If there was any accident and I finished up in a hospital, I would not remember anything. I could see only my feet and walked that way for quite a long time.

Not once did a truck or a car beep me, to my surprise, as I was doing the wrong thing. Step by step, I arrived at another intersection and looking under my cap, I noticed on my right hand side a signpost and reading from the corner of my eyes 'Dumbria'. I was saved, now I had to cross the highway which was so very busy at that time of day. Luckily, I made it, crossing the first two lanes, standing in the middle of the highway before going across the other two lanes. Once more, I had been protected.

In the afternoon, I arrived at the beautiful Dumbria Albergue. At the Albergue, I met two French pilgrims who had started their pilgrimage from Vezelay. It was the first time; I met pilgrims who had started their pilgrimage from this little French village in Bourgogne. What a day!

After a good night's sleep, I left Dumbria for Olveiroa. The path was absolutely gorgeous through forests and fields; the embankments were covered in yellow, purple, white and red poppies. I crossed Celtic villages, I followed roads, and streams, and the birds were singing. It was like being in paradise after what I went through the day before. I am the happiest in nature, with the exception of when I got lost, obviously.

At times, I met pilgrims coming from the opposite direction who helped me to find my way. I arrived at a big intersection called Bifurcacion. Coming from Dumbria, if you turn right you will finish at Cee and then Finisterre, otherwise, go straight towards the village called 'Hospital'. From there, I would walk what I covered in 2010, but in the opposite direction. I was surprised to find out that there was no signage either, if you walked the opposite way. I met some challenges, but not too many as the path was along a main road. I was surprised that walking backwards I could not recognise where I had walked, as I thought I would. I arrived in Olveiroa. I slept in a little house adjacent to the Albergue. Only six or eight bunks, per room, a real luxury and I went for dinner. I returned later on and started to put all my belongings on my bunk, so I could be ready for the next day when Clarisse, from America, entered the room. She bumped me a bit as she was passing close to me, then she realised that she was in the wrong room. I smiled at her and told her not to worry. As she got close to the door, she turned around and sat on my bunk beside me. Clarisse was walking for her Mum who would have been 100 years old in 2018. She had started her pilgrimage with friends but needed to have some time to herself and was walking alone now, though her friends were worried for her as she had Lupus, but she kept in touch with them by phone. She said that she felt I was a nice person.

We engaged in a more private conversation. Clarisse told me that the nuns at Carrion del Condes had given her a medal called 'Miraculous Medal'.

'Claude I am devastated. I have lost it'.

I shared with her what had happened in Leon at the Benedictine Convent when Francoise gave me the medal and that my Maman had been a devotee of Catherine Laboure. Clarisse's emotional suffering was so vivid, that it hurt me and I told her:

'Maybe, I received this medal so I could pass it on to you. I am sure, you should be the recipient'.

Clarisse refused, but the more I insisted, the more she refused. I hugged her, she cried on my shoulder and left.

The next morning, before I was leaving, I had decided to look for Clarisse in the other dormitories. I found her, as she was checking her backpack. I sat on her bunk, held her hand and said:

'Clarisse, I have been thinking during the night. It is not just coincidence that I received this medal. It is for another purpose, this medal was meant for you. I am sure Francoise would agree. This is the Camino with its magic. Please accept the medal with love'.

I took her hand and placed the 'Miraculous Medal', then closed it. Tears ran down her cheeks, and her little body was shaking. For the last time, I hugged her and left, wishing her a 'Buen Camino'. I knew I had done the right thing and took the road. I was at peace with myself.

On the path, there was still no signage, but more pilgrims were walking from Santiago to Finisterre, I was not so stressed, as I had decided that the pilgrims would be my signposts from now on. What did I do when I was in doubt? I waited for the pilgrims to appear from a path, and as soon as I could see one I started walking towards them. As I was walking in the direction of Santa Marina, I stopped two ladies coming towards me so they could take a picture of me on the path. Funnily enough, they were Australians.

At Ponteolveira, crossing the bridge, I was surprised to bump into Thomas from Korea. He was on his way to Finisterre. We had met in Saint-Jean-Pied-de-Port,

France, a town situated at the base of the Pyrenees, 40 days earlier. Thomas told me that the conversation we had there and my wise words had changed his pilgrimage and that he was so happy to have met me again and have the opportunity to tell me and thank me. Though I had no recollection of what I said to him, I was happy to have helped him somehow during his pilgrimage. I stopped at Santa Marina and funnily enough I was staying in the same Albergue where I had stayed in 2010.

The next morning, I was up early. There was, still, no signage and I found myself on a highway again. Across the road I saw a man and I waved at him. With my backpack, who would not have recognised that I was a pilgrim, right? With grand gestures, he showed me the direction to follow. At one stage, after walking along beautiful trail forests, I arrived in a farmland area, and saw three different dirt paths.

Well, which one should I take? I decided to do what our Indigenous trekkers in Australia would have done in my position; I looked at the marks on the trail, as it could have been from locals or pilgrims and honestly, with my leg, I did not fancy walking more kilometres than necessary.

On one of the tracks, there were more marks of boots or maybe jogging shoes going in my direction so I presumed it should be the one I had to take. Amazingly I was right. Ha, ha, I was improving. You can see how it is important not to have sealed roads.

I arrived at Vilaserio. I passed in front of the municipal Albergue situated just at the entrance to the village. It did not feel right and I kept on walking till I saw a sign "Casa Vella". What a blessing! I stopped there. There were hens, roosters, and you could see cows. It was the first time that I felt totally at peace and relaxed, since the beginning of my journey. I met the grandmother who was close to my age. She had opened her house to pilgrims, and now her daughter was running it. It was nearly the end of May, and it was still very cold. In the evening a fire was lit in the fireplace. All the pilgrims from many countries sat around the fire on very comfortable lounge chairs and shared their stories, a reminder of the talks around a wood stove at my Aunt's place when, as a young girl, I was visiting her and her family. During the night there was a huge storm, and the next morning, we saw the devastation in the garden. Sadly, the flower-beds had been damaged and a fig tree had been uprooted.

I left this magical place and took the road again. It was cold, misty and there was heavy rain. I picked up a heart-shaped-stone. I wanted to walk that day for my niece who was battling breast-cancer and many members of my family who are dealing with health issues. Life brings us many challenges and it is the way we handle them that will make the difference.

Each hour of anxiety, doubt, suffering, injustice, joy or victory make us stronger to face our life. Believing and trusting are part of our journey in this modern world of constant doubts.

I crossed many forests. At one stage, I had to cross a stream along a very slippery wooden bridge without handrails. I was hesitant when two German angels arrived to help me. The mist was very dense and I had to follow a main road. I could not see more than a few metres ahead of me. A Dutch lady, who was walking in the opposite direction, stopped me. She needed a listening ear and cried on my shoulder. My heart was so full to have been able to help her in such a simple way. The earth needs the rain to regenerate, maybe we need our tears to grow too, and heal like the rain on a flower and understand the meaning of life. After the rain the sun shines.

At A Pena, I met a young, incredibly courageous, Italian pilgrim. Sandro was walking with half a heart. He needed a heart transplant. Instead of waiting, at home, for a suitable donor, he had decided to walk the Camino. He was in constant contact with his family and his doctors. Sandro was full of hope; nothing would have convinced him otherwise and he was at peace with his decision. He was like a little bird singing along the path touching so many hearts.

More forests, flowers everywhere, gravelly paths, and many more pilgrims on the path. They had become my daily signposts. At one stage, I was unsure which way to take and climbed a little hill. From there I could see the different gravelly paths. I scrutinised the landscape and waited for a pilgrim to appear to find which path I should take to keep on walking without getting lost. It worked all the time.

That day I stopped at Nigreira. I found an Albergue and met two Canadians. I went for my shower and did my chores. I was in agony. I could see Elizabeth looking at me. On my return, Elizabeth approached me and asked what had happened to my leg. I told her that, well before arriving in Santiago, I felt some pain in my leg, but ignored it, until it became very painful which resulted in a shin splint and I had pain in my feet since the early stage of my pilgrimage and I had lost eight toe-nails. Elizabeth could not do much about this, but did some reiki on my leg. It was a godsend.

The next day, I left feeling a bit better. I reached Castelo close to Ames, a little village 12 kilometres from Santiago and found the private lodging 'Casa Riomonte'. I shared a room with three Italian ladies, who told me that the lady of the house was not pleasant at all. I had just arrived at the private lodging when I received a message from Cristele and Bruno, my two French angels, who, in 2010, had picked me up at Sainte-Foy-La-Grande. They had stopped me during my first Camino after a fall down a mountain. They had taken me back to their home so I could have some rest and treatment. At that time, I had been walking so many days on my injured, inflamed knee and displaced pelvis. I never wanted to stop or go to a doctor, as I was sure a doctor would have asked me to stop. Cristele and Bruno had managed to talk sense to me, so I could have treatment. We had kept in contact. They had crossed France and part of Spain with their campervan, so we could meet again. How can anyone be so blessed? After so many years we would meet in a few hours' time.

Needless to say, it was a beautiful reunion. They had parked their campervan close to where I was staying and the lady of the house was not happy, so they had to move it, and the lady told me that I was not allowed to invite my friends to come into the house.

The next morning, the three Italian ladies had left before me. Santiago was only twelve kilometres away. I was going to take my trekking poles where we were asked to leave them, outside the main door, when I realised, that my trekking poles were not there. I rang the bell and informed the owners. I told them that maybe one of the Italian ladies could have taken them by mistake. The wife got angry, saying this had never happened, and told her husband that I was probably lying. I refrained and controlled my frustration saying this was not the case, that there was no reason for me to lie, and left. I had been walking on the road for a little while when I heard a beep. It was coming from a taxi. The three ladies had taken a taxi to reach a certain place that same morning and when they reached their destination and took their backpacks out of the taxi, they realised that one of them had taken my trekking poles by mistake.

The taxi had returned to 'Casa Riomonte' hoping that I would be still there. The owner sent the taxi driver to catch me and had given my description. Well, probably my grey hair and heavy backpack would have given me away. All was well. Honestly, I was hoping this event would be a lesson for the lady of the house. Behind doubts and suspicion there are opportunities to turn things around and learn.

From afar I could see Santiago. It was the same picture that I recorded the first time I looked back at Santiago on my way to Muxia, but this time, I was getting closer to Santiago from a different angle. My feelings were the same as the first two times, and my heart was beating like mad, when I saw at the entrance of Santiago the signpost '0 Km'. It was eleven days, 28 May 2018, after my first entrance to Santiago when I was reunited with the Camino Skies' group. I was back in this magical city and went to my lodging, took possession of my bunk and left. I was going to meet my two French angels, Cristele and Bruno. We were so happy to be able to see each other again. I was in front of the Cathedral, Praza do Obradoiro, when I heard someone calling my name. It was Ernest. We had met at the top of Mount Corpino (Muxia).

He had just arrived in Santiago from walking back along the Dumbria Way, like I did. So the cheeky Claude asked him how he went along the Dumbria Way.

'Claude, there is no signage. I got lost and I had to sleep in the forest one night'.

I replied: 'Oh, dear, I got lost too, but I got out and did not sleep in the forest, fortunately. How good are the oldies?'

We had a good laugh and hugged. I did not share that I walked along a highway forbidden to pedestrians and pilgrims.

My two French angels arrived; we went to visit the Cathedral and Santiago and walked in the city. I wanted to show them that there was a chapel devoted to Catherine Laboure, 'Miraculous Medal'. Believe it or not, I could not find it. I had seen it in 2010. We had dinner and said our good byes not knowing when we would see each other again. It was an emotional moment.

I arrived back at the Albergue, when I saw a lady sitting in an armchair. I had the feeling I had seen her before. She noticed me and was looking at me intensively, as someone you have met before, when suddenly she jumped from the armchair, and at the same moment, we recognized each other. It was Claudia from Germany. The last time we saw each other was after Lorca, some 700 kilometres before Santiago. Claudia said:

'Claude, it is unbelievable. We are leaving the day after tomorrow at 4.00am. Amélie and I were sad as we were leaving without seeing you again and here you are'.

They had just arrived in Santiago. Amélie had been injured. They had to stop along the way until Amélie was able to walk again. We were so happy to see each other again. Amélie was with some friends in a square close to the Albergue. As it was dark I sneaked behind Amélie, put my hands over her eyes and Claudia asked her to guess who was doing that. She jumped laughing, shouting:

'Claude, it is you Claude.'

She took me in her arms. Amélie and I danced on the square like teenagers. What a reunion!

On our way back to the Albergue, Claudia asked me if I remember 'Gerald'. I could not recall and asked her why. They have met him and he was always talking about me along the path. I was somewhat surprised, though I had heard this from the pilgrims I had met previously. Claudia took her mobile out of her pocket, scrolled down and showed me a photo.

'Yes, I remembered him, I replied. I had met Gerald briefly, at a café, just outside Pamplona and since then I had walked close to a 1,000 kilometres'.

Was this a coincidence that Amélie, Claudia and I had met again, just before their return to Germany? Maybe yes, maybe no, maybe there was a reason.

As we walked back, we decided to meet again for breakfast. They took me to an absolutely beautiful place called: 'Casa Vella'. It was the same name as the lodging I had stopped at in Vilaserio a few days before. We were having our breakfast when someone appeared. Yes you guessed right: Gerald! We hugged and finished our breakfast before going each our own way. We had decided to meet again for a last evening meal with some of the pilgrims. They all had met along their pilgrimage. Amélie, a vegan, had difficulty to find proper food, for her, but for me, as a vegetarian, it was easier.

I still had a few days before my return to France, and had decided to walk part of the Portuguese Way and went to the Pilgrims' Office to get some information. I told the attendant that I wanted to walk back from Santiago and finish in a few days somewhere along the Portuguese Camino. I was dissuaded from doing so, as the signage was very poor, many had got lost, and the number of pilgrims walking it backwards was few and far between, and so on.

Well, I had just returned from Muxia. Though it had not always been dramatic, I had been a bit fearful, at times, and without the pilgrims who had become my 'signposts', I could be still walking in the wilderness. I am just joking. Was I becoming wiser? Or was it that the time I had left was too short.

I listened to the advice. I would take a train to Padron, then walk to Herbon and back from Herbon to Padron before walking in Santiago for the third time in a short while. So be it. I returned to the Albergue and asked if I could leave my big backpack with them for a few days as I was going to walk just a few days on the Portuguese Way. They agreed. It was so kind of them. I was putting some clothes in a day pack when I heard someone walking close by. I looked up and to my surprise, who was in front of me? Yes, you guessed it: Gerald.

Gerald was staying at the same Albergue. His bunk's number was 205, mine 206, just above his. Gerald informed me that he would come and pick me up by 7.00pm.

'I will take you to the restaurant where we would meet Amélie, Claudia and all the other pilgrims'.

I thanked him and kept on checking which clothes I would take to walk along the Portuguese Camino. Gerard left. That same night, at dinner, I was going to meet some new pilgrims who were to become part of my Camino Family such as Aida, Anja and others.

The next morning, I was climbing down the ladder hoping not to awaken Gerald, but it did not work and Gerald suggested having breakfast together, to which I agreed. We went to a café just across the Albergue, a young male with Down's syndrome was looking after the patrons and I asked the management if this young man could serve us. He gave me a beautiful smile and thanked me.

While having breakfast, Gerald opened up. During the conversation, I said to him that I have met a lot of pilgrims along the Camino Frances who mentioned to me that a male pilgrim was always talking about me on the path and I was wondering if it is him. He replied to the affirmative and told me that we met on April 15th 2018 and this day will stay in his heart forever. I had hugged him and through my hug he felt so much energy and that hug had changed his life forever. After our meeting, his Camino changed and every single day, he talked about me to all the pilgrims he crossed paths with. He had come to the Camino, as he wanted to connect with people and after our hug, he did.

Gerald's words touched me to the deepest part of my soul. I knew about the power of a hug, I had been told by pilgrims, people I had met during the course of my life, what they had felt after this simple exchange, but there was some 'je ne sais quoi' about Gerald's words which resonated more. I had helped another human being and I was hearing this beautiful comment in Santiago, like in 2010. I felt so blessed. I had collected a heart-shaped-stone somewhere between Muxia-Dumbria and Santiago. I had kept it waiting to find out who I should give to. After our sharing, I knew. I took it out of my bag and gave it to Gerald. It was the last heart-shaped-stone I would give, I thought.

We went back to the Albergue, collected our backpack and walked down the road, holding hands, and separated. Gerald was going towards the bus station and I, the train station, both in different directions. Gerald will remain a friend, forever, and he is part of my Camino family.

As I arrived at the train station, it started to rain a bit. I checked the time-table and noticed that I had made a mistake; the wait for the train was more than two hours. I decided to leave the train station and wait somewhere else.

The rain got a little bit heavier and I stopped at a café and ordered a hot chocolate drink. A few minutes later, the waiter brought my hot chocolate, a croissant and four small pieces of cakes. I told him that I never ordered that, he answered: "I know it is from us to you". Stunned, I thanked him.

The magic of Santiago was continuing. I was revisiting in my mind the last events on my second Camino, when I decided to write something in my journal and went through my diary back to April 15th. I could not believe it and read:

"Met Gerald, from the Netherlands, a lot of energy through a hug"

It was the first and last time I wrote something like that in my diary.

On April 15, I had met Kathie and Douglas who were walking for a charity dear to their hearts, collecting money to get young girls and boys out of prostitution in India. Harrison, then I met his wife in Burgos, Amélie, Claudia, Alexander and Gerald. It will be a day to remember, always, for the rest of my life.

Sunset at Muxia - Spain

The Itinerary: 10 Days Finisterre – Muxia – Dumbria – Santiago de Compostela

Day	From	To
1	Finisterre	Lires
2	Lires	Muxia
3	Muxia	Dumbria
4	Dumbria	Olveiroa
5	Olveiroa	Santa Marina
6	Marina	Vilaserio
7	Vilaserio	A Pena
8	A Pena	Negreira
9	Negreira	Ames
10	Ames	Santiago

CHAPTER 5

Walking alone in Spain and Portugal

Herbon – Padron – Santiago de Compostela

3 days: 30 May 2018 - 1 June 2018
at 72 years of age.

Visiting, walking and travelling in and around Fatima – Porto

5 days: 2 June 2018 - 6 June 2018
at 72 years of age.

The train took me to Padron, and I started to walk towards Herbon. I was still walking without a map, a guide-book or a GPS. When I was halfway between Herbon and Padron, I decided to return to Padron and find lodging. I had no luck; even the sales assistants in the shops did not know about any Albergue which was very surprising, knowing the importance of Padron in the story of Saint James.

I stopped asking in the shops and kept on walking along the main road when I saw, across the street, a couple, who did not have a backpack, but somehow I felt that they were pilgrims. I met Alicia and Hugh, from Ireland, who suggested I come with them to where they were staying. As we arrived at their lodging, quite a few pilgrims entered. I told them to go first. As they registered and left, the receptionist informed me that there were no more rooms available. I asked her to check a bit better. It was cold and I did not fancy sleeping outside. I think she felt pity for me and said that they have a room under the attic that they never let it because it is not great, but… I did not let her finish and told her not to worry: I will take it. To me, it was just so beautiful, especially after sleeping in dormitories. I felt like a queen and light-hearted, I went to the Church of Saint James of Padron, neo-classical style, dating back to the 10th century and saw a sign: 'Albergue for pilgrims'. Ha ha ha!

Padron is a suburb of Iria Flavia. If you follow the Christian Tradition, it is there that the boat was moored, carrying Saint-James' dead body after his beheading. There are many Jacobean oil paintings in the church as well as 'The Pedron' which is a

Roman altar stone believed to be the stone where the Apostle's boat was moored. Back at my lodging, I met an Australian deacon from Sydney and many other pilgrims from various nations.

The next day, I left early towards Gandalas. The path was mostly on roads, through the countryside and I crossed some hamlets with their typical Celtic houses. When I arrived at the Albergue, there was only one bunk left. I had to enter through such a small space, it felt like if I was going into a 'rabbit hole'. Going in or out was not easy at all, especially for a 72 year-old woman. Christine from Germany and I had a good laugh as I said:

'I hope there is no camera here'.

She left and returned with a packet of Camomile tea bags. I was touched by her gesture and thanked her.

The next morning was going to be the last day for me on the Portuguese Camino. The path was, again, mostly along the roads, with very little space to walk between the roads and pavements allocated to pedestrians. From the road, on the outskirts of a town, I could see a forest and could not work out why; there was no path there for the pilgrims when it was so dangerous for us to walk on the side of the road. Thank God, it was not a highway!! I remembered the naughty thing I did to reach Dumbria.

I was thinking about that when I saw some pilgrims coming down a hill on the right hand side of the road. I was very surprised to see so many and thought that I must have missed a 'blue arrow'. I should not complain if I had to walk along the road. I was surprised as well as the arrow in front of me was indicating straight ahead. I walked for a while when something told me to walk back where I had seen all these pilgrims coming down the steep street. I had time so I went back and did so. As I arrived at the top of the hill, I noticed that the street was leading to a church, well to me, more a chapel than a church called 'Saint Mary Magdalena', built in 1456.

I entered and met Estella who showed me around and explained the history of this little chapel. Behind the altar, in a secure box, there is the sculpture of a woman lying down representing Saint Mary Magdalena and below her in a box a tiny piece of her bone. I was wandering around the little chapel, taking a photo of Mary Magdalene's painting when, by accident; I bumped into a young man and met

David from Manchester. In front of the painting, I told David that in 2010, I started my first pilgrimage from Vezelay in Northern Central France where Saint Mary Magdalena's Basilica was built during the 11th Century. Vezelay is one of the four routes in France the pilgrims have to take, if they want to walk the Saint James' Way across France.

There you can see some remains of Mary Magdalena in a magnificent wrought-iron casket as well. I told him how strange it was that I felt I had to walk back this morning to come to this chapel. He was listening to me very attentively, and took my arm as he wanted me to meet a friend of his.

I followed him and met Gavin, a young priest from the outskirts of Manchester, England. David and Gavin were walking the Portuguese Camino. David asked me to tell Gavin what I had just told him a few minutes before. As I was sharing my story Gavin was listening with attention and looked at me with astonishment. Gavin has been ordained on 22 July 2017 which is Saint Mary Magdalena's feast day. She is his protector. One year after Gavin's ordination, on 22 July 2018, he will give a very special blessing to celebrate his first year as a priest. I informed, Gavin, it is marvellous and I will be thinking of him on that day.

I asked him if he could add my name to the other parishioners that day as it would be a special blessing after his one year ordination.

He replied: 'Claude, you will be there in front of me, you will be the first one I give this blessing to and you know what I will give it to you today'.

After this special blessing, Gavin said a mass and I stayed for it. What a special moment in my life! After the mass, I left this little chapel, thinking about if I had not listened to my instinct; I would have missed an opportunity to receive another special blessing in my life.

How many times have we not listened to our heart and intuition? How many times have we missed something which would have changed the course of our life, out of fear or not trusting our inner-self as we were not confident enough or did not have courage or strength to speak up? How many opportunities have we missed for growth? How many opportunities had I received during my lifetime to turn things around! Behind chaos and obstacles sometimes things fall into place as if by magic.

With these thoughts, I kept on walking across forests, hamlets, bridges, and walked along streams. I was wondering if I had done the full circle with the Camino, I started my first Camino from the Basilica of Saint Mary Magdalena, in 2010, and on that day in 2018, I was finishing my Caminos and stopped at this little Chapel named Saint Mary Magdalena. I was in my thoughts when I reached a point indicating two ways to reach Santiago. I was pondering which one I should take when Gavin and David caught up to me. We walked together for maybe one kilometre, and then they went ahead. Talk about youth! They were walking too fast, for an oldie like me!

Coming from Portugal, you enter at a different point in Santiago than if you arrived from Muxia or Finisterre or the Camino Frances. I saw the Cathedral from afar. This was indicating the end of my pilgrimage for 2018. Seeing it, my feelings were different from the ones I had when I finished my first Camino, the second and third time just a few weeks ago. I was downhearted and sad, but it was a different type of sadness. I could not quite comprehend it. I stopped at a Plaza, and sat on some stairs, when I was joined by Christine that I met the day before at the Albergue of Gandalas. Christine would not enter Santiago alone and she was very happy. My sadness disappeared too, not to think about it ever. We took the traditional photo in front of the Cathedral and went each our own way. We were staying at different Albergues. I was putting my raincoat on the bunk when I checked my pocket and found a banana. I did not know which angel had put it there, but sent a kiss to the Universe and the person who could have made this lovely gesture. I presumed it was Christine.

There were so many train strikes in France that I had to modify my plans for returning to France and went to the Pilgrims' Office to find another option. There was a travel agent beside the Pilgrims' Office and I was advised to fly out of Porto. Well, in that case, I will go to Fatima.

In the afternoon, I was hanging my clothes in the Albergue courtyard, in Santiago, when I saw a young lady deep in thoughts. I could feel how heavy her heart was. I waited a few minutes, then sat beside her and waited. This is the way I met Maureen from America. Eventually, Maureen opened up and once more I became a listening ear. We all walked the Camino for our own personal reasons. If we are ready to receive the messages, if our heart is open, during our pilgrimage, we will revisit, like a movie, the bad, the good, the very bad, the very good we have lived and as well what we have done, what we should have done and so on. The pilgrimage will show us the way to make amends. If we do that, we will return anew and live the life we are supposed to live with a lighter heart. Maureen was struggling and I asked her to wait for me. I went to look for my backpack. Somewhere between Padron and Gandalas I had seen a heart-shaped-stone and picked it up. I returned to Maureen and gave it to her, hoping that she would find peace in her heart before returning to America. I have to say that I met many American women walking the Portuguese Way.

In the evening, Gavin and David arrived at the Albergue where I was staying at. Gavin had participated in the mass at the Cathedral at 7.30pm. He was over the moon and I was so happy for him. I informed him that I would be going to Fatima, before flying out from Porto. Gavin asked me to pray for him and think about him in Fatima, and I eagerly promised to do that.

The next day, I travelled eight hours by bus to reach Fatima. In the bus, I had met two American ladies and we had a bit of chit-chat. We decided to share a taxi that would take us to two different Albergues.

Later in the afternoon, I visited Fatima briefly before assisting at the outdoor mass in front of the large Basilica and sanctuary. It is a very impressive place. I wanted to participate in the procession, and bought some candles for my whole family and for my very special friends back in Brisbane and in France, especially for Jeannette, as she has pushed me to write. If I had not listened to her, I would have missed so much of what life was offering me.

I was listening to the Mass when I started to feel like fainting. I apologized in English to a couple standing beside me. The lady replied in English and asked me if I had a bottle of some water. I shook my head in the affirmative and she told me to drink some quickly. Brett and Robyn took me to a seat and after drinking some water, I felt better. I had realised that they had an Australian accent, and asked them if they were from Australia? They were. Believe it or not, Brett and Robyn lived on the outskirts of Brisbane, Australia, where I live. They visit Fatima every year. I was able to do the procession and walk back to my lodging. I had been blessed once more.

The next morning, it was cold and raining. However, I went to walk the Way of the Cross where the apparition of the Virgin Mary had occurred and where the children, Jacinta and Francisco Marto, Lucia Dos Santos were born at the little village of Aljustrel. In the afternoon I visited the Basilica and listened to an amazing live recital before visiting the Sanctuary of Our lady of Fatima.

On my way back to the Albergue, I sat on a bench and met an Italian-Brazilian woman, Patricia. She had lived in Italy for twenty-four years and had two young children. Her Italian ex-husband was always smacking and screaming at the children, to the point that she had to leave. At the present time, her children were with her mother in Brazil, as Patricia could not find any work in her birth country. Her heart was broken as she lives and works in Portugal away from her family due to economic circumstances. She was sending most of her money back to Brazil for the care and upkeep of her children.

In doing so, she had to live in a shelter to save some money, with very little hope that one day she would be able to see her children again before they grew up.

I walked back to the Albergue, full of questions? What are we doing in our society? How can we let this happen? Where are our responsibilities? What can we do to prevent such things? How many in the world have to leave their country to find work and send money to their family back home? This was quite current in the 20th century after the Second World War, but now in 2018! Patricia's heart was broken, she had no other choice. I found that she was so brave. I do not think I could have had her courage, living away from my children.

It was raining when I left. Kindly, the owner of the Albergue where I was staying drove me to the bus station. A few hours later, I was in Porto and started to visit the city. I was in awe with Porto, its Cathedral, its public gardens, its monuments, its buildings, its houses covered in tiles with amazing designs and colours, and most of its people.

After walking a few hours, I returned to my lodging, which was a private Albergue. I was sitting on my bunk, looking at my three trekking poles. I could not have re-entered Australia with them due to the

Government rules and decided to leave them at the municipal Albergue which was at the other side of the city, for another pilgrim to use.

After breakfast, I embarked on finding the municipal Albergue. I asked at the reception where it was. With a list of the streets, I started my journey across the city. Five hours later, tired, I was still looking for the municipal Albergue. I had stopped and asked many locals where the municipal Albergue was. Once I had reached a certain point. I was sent in the other direction. In the end, I had had enough and thought: you are tired, you have been sent left and right from one side of the city to the other without success. I made the decision that I will enter the first church I see and leave the trekking poles near the altar with a note, if there was no priest around.

A little while later, at the top of a street, I saw a lovely church covered with blue tiles and entered. There were a few people in the church, but no priest. I started to write, on a piece of paper, in English, my wishes for the trekking poles, when I saw a young girl taking some photos inside the church. I had noticed her when she was walking in the street. On her backpack it was written 'Planet'.

I approached her and asked her if she was a pilgrim. Natalie replied that she was. I asked her if she had any trekking poles. Natalie shook her head in the negative. I pulled out of my backpack the three trekking poles and gave them to her. Natalie was from Israel and was starting her first day on the Camino. Tears rolled down her cheeks, as a stranger had shown some kindness to her. In fact, it was really nothing. I hugged her and she cried on my shoulder. As I went out of the church, I was stopped by a couple who had witnessed our interactions. They told me: how magical this moment was for them too. It was going to be the last blessing of my Camino in 2018 and my heart was full.

I flew first to France and then to England spending some time with my families in these two countries, where I was spoiled, before returning to Australia.

A question remains for me: will I be able to return to the Camino? Well, let us see what the future holds!

Once a pilgrim on the Camino, always a pilgrim on the Camino.

My life since my early childhood has not been an easy one, but I am grateful for my experiences so I can now help others.

Camino Portugues - Portugal

The Itinerary: 3 Days
Herbon – Padron – Gandalas – Santiago de Compostela

Day	From	To
1	Herbon	Padron
2	Padron	Gandalas
3	Gandalas	Santiago

The Itinerary: 5 Days
Visiting, walking and travelling in and around Fatima – Porto

I would like to share with you this prayer, written by a Franciscan monk named Dino, who has lived in the village of 'La Faba' prior to O'Ceibrero. I saw it when I was in the little church of Mary Magdalena on the Portuguese Way. To me it summarises our Camino. I will leave you with these words.

Though I have crossed all the Way

Crossed mountains and valleys

From East up to West

If I have not discovered the freedom of being myself

I have gotten nowhere

Though I had shared all my goods

With people of another language and culture

Made friendships with pilgrims of thousand paths

or shared lodging with saints and princes

If I am not able to forgive my neighbor tomorrow

I have gotten to nowhere.

Tadapani Village: 2,675 mn - Nepal

CHAPTER 6

Walking alone or with a group?

Trekking, walking long distances, alone or in a group: the pros and cons. I can only speak from my own experiences which are very limited and the type of hiking or long distances you want to do.

Claude on the Camino Frances

Larapinta Trail - Australia

WALKING ALONE.

You will have a free mind, leaving time for your sense of freedom to fly exponentially.

You can connect more with nature and contemplate, live the moment.

If you cross paths with people you will be ready for others and you may have more precious meetings which will be invaluable memories.

You will never have the feeling of being rushed. However, at times, you can be caught by loneliness if you do not meet anyone for many days or weeks, but you can spend more time taking photos without feeling guilty about slowing down the group.

You will learn to be more resilient and discover your strength and the real you.

The downside is if you get hurt, you have only yourself to rely on. Also, you will need to carry your heavy backpack all the way.

A little advice: if you decide to walk alone, message a member of your family or a friend daily informing them where you are and where you would like to finish that day.

WALKING WITH A GROUP.

Members of the group can walk faster or slower than you, putting pressure on you and the group. This means that you will have to push yourself more or maybe walk longer hours than you want. This can create some stress in you and compromise your sense of freedom.

You will have to walk the distance planned. If you are too tired or exhausted, you have to keep on going until you reach your destination or try to keep pace.

In a group, as you may not know the members, you will have to deal with people who have different views or see you differently from what you are, because of the way they see themselves or from the environment for which they have been born or raised. It is not easy as for any human being as most of our beliefs are limited and some can be very judgmental.

The other side of the coin is that if you find someone you can connect with, you will have a new friend forever. You will always eat in company. If you get hurt you will have someone with you.

I do understand that going to a country where you do not know the language is challenging and in a way you can find it safer to travel or walk with a group.

If you feel uncomfortable travelling by yourself, then travelling with a group is for you.

Your decision to walk with a group or alone is yours only. There is no right or wrong.

Personally, after experiencing walking alone and with groups, I prefer to walk alone.

Remember, the choice is yours and yours only. Do not let your fear stop you from doing what you want.

While working as a volunteer in palliative care and cancer wards in Brisbane, I came to realise that most people's biggest regret in their dying days is when they did not do something because of their fear.

In this world of fears we need to turn our greatest challenges into our greatest strengths. Negative thoughts take us along the wrong path.

Every individual is responsible for his or her own choices, and actions. I am not saying that is easy either.

Each person has to find his or her personal answers regarding his or her life.

Life is a long stretch of road, sometimes flat or nearly flat, sometimes going uphill, as if we are climbing Mount Everest, sometimes downhill, sometimes peaceful like a flat open space.

Life can be boring at times and exciting at others: live the moment!

Every challenge, you have met or will meet, is placed in front of you so you can grow, become a better person, be the person you should be so you can live your life purpose. Life is challenging at times, more than what you thought you could bear; but eventually you will discover that it was a blessing in disguise.

Listen to your inner-voice. Be courageous and look for the blessing.

Remember, we are never alone.

Learn to respect everyone, look for the good in people you meet, you won't always see it at first but with love and a peaceful mind, your path on this earth will be lighter and the blessing will reveal itself.

If you have faith, your life and its discovery will be easier. Try to see light and love in the worst moments in your life so you can find some happiness and, peacefulness. If you can't see it because your heart is so torn just take the road and walk in a park or a forest, look, observe nature: this is our teacher.

Our last destination is death. What is important: it is what happened between birth and death!

This is your journey. Do not waste your life: live life, embrace life, love life. Be happy.

Live the life you are meant to live.

Have a great journey!

3rd time back to Santiago de Compostela - Spain in 14 days

EPILOGUE

It is hard for me to think and comprehend why we have to fight each other through wars, thoughts, ideas, when we have so much in common as spiritual beings or atheists, as we are one. Our earthly feelings are the same, deep down; we are all looking for love, understanding, connection, peace with one another without discrimination as we are all connected.

Our disconnection with ourselves and the world has created the mayhem we are living in. It is maybe time for future generations to revive our universal consciousness, so they can live in a better world with more understanding and sharing.

If all over the globe, the hand of forgiveness is extended, and egos are put aside, each side can look ahead as one and our world will live in peace. It cannot happen quickly, but one step at a time; hand in hand it can be achieved with will and strength of character.

Love is the only way to stop the suffering of our world. I hope that one day eventually, love will enter everyone heart. Then there is a possibility that the darkness of life will be lifted and a new radiant, dazzling day will be born. The colours of the flowers will be brighter, the songs of the birds happier, sharper.

We, as human beings walking on this planet, will be able to sing and leave fear behind us. Maybe it is a utopian dream, but why not? Every change that has happened on this planet started with one person, one thought could lead to action. Even in our personal life we can change the course of our life with a foot step and at time baby steps. We need to start somewhere, sometime, why not now?

ACKNOWLEDGEMENT

I would like to thank Dr. Maureen Bella, Mrs. Robyn Wilson, Miss Tracey Laing my readers for their support, trust, advice, constant love, and friendship.

God bless you all.